Homemade·ish

Homemade·ish

Recipes and Cooking Tips
That Keep It Real

Recipes and Photographs by

Lauren McDuffie

Gibbs Smith

First Edition
28 27 26 25 24   5 4 3 2 1

Published by
Gibbs Smith
570 N. Sportsplex Dr.
Kaysville, Utah 84037

1.800.835.4993 orders
www.gibbs-smith.com

Designed by Sheryl Dickert
Production design by Renee Bond
Printed and bound in China

Library of Congress Control Number: 2023950741
ISBN: 978-1-4236-6567-0

This product is made of FSC®-certified and other controlled material.

To home cooks everywhere.

Contents

Hello, Home Cook

We've likely never met but if I may be so bold, I'd be willing to bet we have a few things in common. Firstly, and maybe most importantly, I'm guessing you enjoy food. I'm also going to wager a guess that you'd rather be almost anywhere other than standing in front of a pile of dirty dishes, just waiting to be washed. I'm guessing you're busy, and that you sometimes find yourself wishing there were more hours in the day to get it all done. Furthermore, I'll bet you don't love wasting money on food that sits around untouched because you didn't have time or energy to get to the cooking of it. These, incidentally, are facts of life, their truths reverberating through our days whether we like them to or not. It seems to be growing ever harder to reconcile all of these facts, and it was their pesky presence that ultimately led me right here, to this book and my great hope that I can lend some relief, at least where dinner is concerned.

Though I adore cooking and the occasional challenging kitchen project, thick with technique and quirky ingredients that require wild goose–chasing just to locate, most of the time I just want my cooking to be as efficient and effective as possible.

Actually, let me begin again, a few steps back. Before I began my career in the food world, I worked in government. My time and efforts were largely spent learning and working to find the fastest, most budget-sensitive, most impactful methods to accomplish . . . well, just about everything. Fast-forward to today, and though my work is very different than it once was, I still find these principles of efficiency and effectiveness taking precedence in all the work I do, their value undeniable.

I run a website called *My Kitchen Little* that is devoted to providing my fellow home cooks with recipes, ideas, inspiration, tips, and tricks to help get dinner on the table with ease and efficiency, without sacrificing the enjoyment of it all, the "effectiveness." I'm always tweaking ingredients and methods to try and find the version that best meets these ends. The primary goal, however, is to get more people in the kitchen cooking homemade food and sharing it, either with an exclusive party of one (I love solo dining) or a big, bustling table of many.

To me, time spent in the kitchen is time filled with opportunity. We get this chance each day to fuel and nourish ourselves and our people. Whether you dine at a table in a formal space, at a kitchen island, or in recliners with TV trays, home cooking points us toward one another, toward ourselves. It keeps us moving in the right direction.

Can takeout and delivery do this? Yeah, sure. But what those types of eating lack are the care and time that went into the making of it. When you've made something yourself, it just hits different. It carries greater impact, always. Even if it's the simplest, most humble thing, cobbled together from what you had in your pantry. When food comes to life in a home kitchen, we're more thoughtful about, and thankful for, what we're eating. We take our time with it, ensuring that appreciation and attention hold their ground.

Time spent creating and enjoying home-cooked food is time well spent. Full stop. This is where we do our best living. We grow, and share, and learn, and fight, and heal, and connect. But sometimes, we're busy—almost too busy to be bothered with the task of cooking, with the work of it all.

How do we reconcile the impact and importance of providing home cooked meals with the ever-lurking busyness that threatens to send us dashing to our doors to answer the call of our latest food deliveries? What do we do about this? Where's the hatch?

Homemade-ish

Somewhere between totally scratch cooking and restaurant-made fare exists this easy, breezy in-between place where food can be anything you want it to be. There are no stuffy rules or trying-too-hard trends, no pretenses to uphold. It's about showing up, not showing off—because that's what matters, that's what people hold on to.

Recipes can satisfy more than just a craving. This book was designed to help satisfy our desires to get rid of unnecessary stress and to get back our precious time. Let's spend less of it tending to the tedium of preparation, of cleanup. Let's spend more of it around the table, enjoying the bits and bites of delicious fare that we made. Did we make it from scratch? Nope. But we made it possible, and that counts for so very much. **That's** what it's all about. At the literal end of the day, the whole goal is often to be together, to be still and present. To just Be.

This book was created to help us get there.

Meant to be a place of comfort, this book is an invitation to let your hair down and relax a little. No judging. No pretenses. Just simple, unfussy food that you really can throw together in minutes, whenever the need may arise. Quietly cheering you on, encouraging you from one page to the next, *Homemade-ish* is here to be your supportive guide, a trusty companion in this busy, bustling world in which our lives spin madly from one day to the next. A delicious devotional of sorts, every recipe a reminder to take it easy on yourself, to keep it real.

No, you really don't have to make the stock from scratch, or the pesto, or even the mashed potatoes. No, there is nothing wrong with using a store-bought pizza crust, or doctoring up a boxed cake mix, or bagged salad.

No, you don't have to be practically perfect in every way. There's no such thing, and don't let anyone tell you otherwise.

So, let's quiet the riot, turn down all of that needless noise. Instead, let's work to increase the fun and the savoring—of more than just the bites we take, but of the time we spend being truly present, with others and with ourselves. Breaking away from the monotonous, stressful, and pressure-laden dinner routine is a great way to do that, and these recipes are here to help. They'll help get dinner on the table faster and with less fuss. They'll keep you from having to spend an hour washing dishes.

But what I hope most of all, is that they'll give you plenty of new ideas and a sustained sense of motivation to keep the momentum going, long after you've had your fill of these pages. I hope to instill in you, fellow home cook, a sense of confidence and an inner conviction that whispers "Yes, I can do that. I can make this recipe."

Less "I give up," and more "I've got this."
Less "I have to be the best," more "I'm doing my best."
Less "I have to make dinner" and more "I want to make dinner."
Less labor, more love.

This is dinnertime at its brightest, at its best. But even at its most basic, it should make you feel good. Or even just . . . not bad. I'll take a neutral dinnertime experience, sure. But it is my primary hope that these recipes will breathe some freshness into your routine, give you new highly doable foods for thought. Consider this to be a book of encouragement, more than 100 love notes from busy me to busy you, to aid in the worthy pursuit of those things.

We Hold These Truths To Be Shelf-Evident:

No one cares if you use homemade chicken stock.
Stouffer's lasagna is very good.
Garlic powder is a thing of beauty and a joy forever.

Canned beans. Canned beans!

Frozen peas and puff pastry are nice to have around at all times.

Premade curry pastes are to be revered, magical workhorses that they are.

At the end of the day, it's how you make people feel. Satisfied. Cared for, cared about. Even if "people" is just you. No one cares if you made the dough from scratch, if the meal is five courses or just one. Most people don't seem to ever mind, let alone notice, if their meal came from a bag or a can, the freezer, or the garden. No one is keeping score, no one is judging you.

With this book, I'm sharing dozens of recipes that are really just permission slips in delicious disguise. With every store-bought shortcut and quick-fix trick, I'm giving you the freedom to cut yourself some slack. Because we're all just doing our best, right? We're tired, but even so, we're out here trying. If we can shape-shift a monotonous daily "chore" into something better, more fun, then we've made it sticky—we've given it staying power. Homemade food can stand its ground as a positive, permanent fixture in our everydays. Something we might even look forward to, rather than wanting to run away from . . . right into the open arms of our food delivery drivers.

But again, to keep it up, we have to keep it real.

Philosophy

1. While I by no means believe that every element—or even most elements—of a meal need to be made from scratch, I also don't think that ordering takeout or simply opening bags of frozen this and boxes of frozen that each night is good for us. So, *Homemade-ish* recipes hover somewhere in the middle. Minimalist by design, each recipe here leans on helpful and time-saving store-bought ingredient(s) that we'll transform into something entirely new, something fun, and far more interesting.

2. No matter what the meal actually is, if you made it yourself—brought it to life in your own kitchen—you're already doing a world of good simply by being there. **You** get to control the scene; **you** get to call the shots. Nothing passes without your approval, and, because of this, you're avoiding the consumption of hidden ingredients or sneaky amounts of naughty things. Sure, dining out and heating up frozen things is easy, and it can taste really great, but largely, that's due to the abandon with which restaurant cooks and food manufacturers add ingredients to make food taste that way, and to make it last for a long time on store shelves and on your shelves. So, preparing your meals at home and being selective about which convenience or premade items you implement will always be the healthiest option.

3. For this to work, for *Homemade-ish* cooking to really be sustainable, it needs to fuel us properly, it should nourish us and fill us with things we can feel good about eating. While the packaged food industry has come a **long** way in the past couple of decades, for a *Homemade-ish* recipe to really be worth its salt (literally), it requires a strong assist from the produce department. As such, most of these recipes will also contain whole, fresh ingredients—vegetables, fruits, healthy oils, green herbs. It's all about balance, finding ways to create fast and easy dishes with little fuss, while also avoiding the consumption of questionable, sketchy things that might not serve us so well. Save for the desserts, we'll be walking that line from the first recipe to the last.

Shop Around

Grocery shopping. We either love it or hate it, don't we? I tend to fall squarely in the latter camp, the whole experience often filling me with a sense of dread. Between us, it's just not my favorite excursion. Either way, dinner usually starts in the aisles of our local markets, be they super or not. But recently, as I've worked my way through this book, I've gained a renewed appreciation for my local grocery store, and just how much help they're offering me every single time I step inside. I'd just been looking at it wrong.

Am I trying to convince you that after reading this book, walking through the automatic doors into your supermarket will suddenly reveal a Narnia of food options, with magical woodland creatures just waiting to assist you through a perfect, worry-free shopping experience? No, that's not really my goal here. Rather, I just want to pass along simple-yet-effective hacks that I've learned, things that truly uplift the food shopping experience into one that is actually kind of . . . fun.

The trick here, is all in how you view it. Sure it's just a bunch of aisles with cans and bottles and jars and boxes of this and that. But that's just the surface level. Adjust your vision a little bit, dive just a little deeper, and it turns out some of those things are treasures hiding in plain sight, waiting for us to dust them off and give them a new shine.

That jar of pesto? It's dying to be transformed into the secret ingredient in some killer meatballs.

The jar of pickled Italian vegetables? It's going to make the most wonderful skillet of spicy, tangy pork tenderloin you've ever tried.

And sure, that crispy, already-fried chicken in your grocer's deli section is probably pretty great (it usually is), but it can be even better when slathered in a maple cream sauce and perched atop some waffled cornbread.

It really is about looking for what these items can do **for** you, rather than what you **have** to do with them. Sure, these recipes are asking you to do specific things with specific ingredients, but they also contain suggestions as to how to change them up, to freestyle on your own terms if you like. These recipes contain multitudes, they really do.

Maybe, by the time you've cooked your way through these pages, you'll have gained a new perspective on grocery shopping, too. Hopefully, you'll see those store shelves in a new, more appealing light.

Some Things Worth Noting

- I'm a food stylist and photographer, and I have a room in my home dedicated to storing the sizable collection of cookware, serveware, gadgets, and gizmos I've amassed over years of working in food. But, to double down on my point here, and to really walk the walk, I'm only going to use and therefore photograph these recipes in the small collection of dishes and serveware that I actually use in my "real life." You really don't need a bunch of fancy equipment, serving pieces, or stuffy, single-use tools to consistently prepare and serve great meals. So, this is me cooking for real, and sharing these dishes with you as I would if you were to come to my house (which, incidentally, is where I've shot the whole book). This is me, keeping it real.

- Furthermore, you can make everything in this book with these 13 kitchen tools:

a cutting board	large baking sheets	a large spatula or spoon
a chef's knife	a muffin pan	a blender/food processor
a large/deep lidded pot	a Dutch oven	a strainer/colander
a large skillet	a grater	
a medium lidded pot	a can opener	

- Every ingredient in this book can be found at a standard supermarket (as confirmed by my trusty recipe testers, who reside from sea to shining sea).

- No recipe requires more than about 20-ish minutes of your hands-on time.

- You're going to need to have **salt, pepper, olive oil, and butter** around at all times. Those things are as essential to cooking as, say, your pots and pans. They're all-the-time things, our ride-or-die crew.

All right then. With that, let's get cooking.

Things Your Grocer's Meat Department Will Do For You
(so you don't have to)

There is much freedom to be found in knowing there are people in your grocery store who are waiting—wanting, even—to help you in your cooking endeavors. I'm not talking about specialty stores or high-end markets, either. Every supermarket in America (and beyond) staffs and trains people who are ready and able to do so much more than retrieving chicken breasts or stuffed pork loins from behind the glass cases. These people are treasure troves of butchery knowledge and skill and I'm just not sure everyone knows this or takes full advantage of it. So, here I am spreading that grocery gospel once again. While you go about your shopping, checking off one item after another, the squad of butchery-focused folk behind the meat counter can be going to work for you in a number of helpful, time-saving ways. While they can't always fulfill your request on the spot, typically (if you ask nicely) they will take care of you in a timely manner. And since knowledge is so very often its own form of power, consider this small-yet-mighty list a supercharger for your supermarket routine.

Spatchcocking, or deboning • This refers to the removal of the chicken's backbone, a step that yields a very flat (i.e. even-cooking) bird that really does cook up beautifully as a result. While doing this really isn't hard, the easiest way to spatchcock your chicken is to 1) Either find one that has already been done, which is fairly common. 2) Simply ask someone behind your store's meat/butcher counter to do it for you.

Dividing larger pieces of meat • Maybe you need a big beef tenderloin cut and tied into perfect filets mignons. Or, maybe you need a chicken or big turkey cut into individual pieces. Or, maybe a brisket or a prime rib, a rack of ribs, or even lamb. The breaking down, portioning, and repackaging of cumbersome meats of all makes and models is a very handy time and labor-saving task that your store's butchers will always take off your literal hands.

Repackage an item according to how much you need • Speaking of repackaging, your grocer's butcher will also rearrange any prepackaged meats to better suit your needs. Let's say you have a romantic pork chop meal for two planned (this is a thing, I'm sure), but can only find them in packs of four or more. The folks behind that meat counter will remove those chops, give you the two that you want, and wrap them back up with a shiny new (cheaper) price tag to boot. All you have to do is ask.

Cooking advice • This is my favorite, actually. You may not necessarily need to order anything unique at the meat counter, or even have them do anything specific with the meat on hand, but what I think most people don't take near enough advantage of is the knowledge that the butcher counter teams possess. The fact that you can mosey up to the counter with nary an idea as to what to do with any of the displayed items and leave with an entire dinnertime plan and knowledge base is charming to me. It's got a nice old-school feel to it, this basic exchange of ask-and-answer information between shopper and grocer.

Prepping • From trussing and pounding chicken and even seasoning or marinating it, to "frenching" lamb chops, carving crown roasts of pork and standing rib roasts, the people behind the butcher counter can move you several steps closer to the dinnertime finish line.

Special order • Whether you realize it or not, when you step up to the gleaming glass butcher case at your supermarket, the whole world o' meat is really your oyster. You aren't restricted to just what they happen to have available when you walk up, but rather, you are only limited by your own imagination. From trotters and whole geese to quail and organic, free-range Cornish game hens, supermarket butcher counters will typically order anything you want, so long as you're cool with waiting for it to arrive. Bonus? These items are usually less expensive when ordered at a supermarket butcher counter, as opposed to a pricier specialty store.

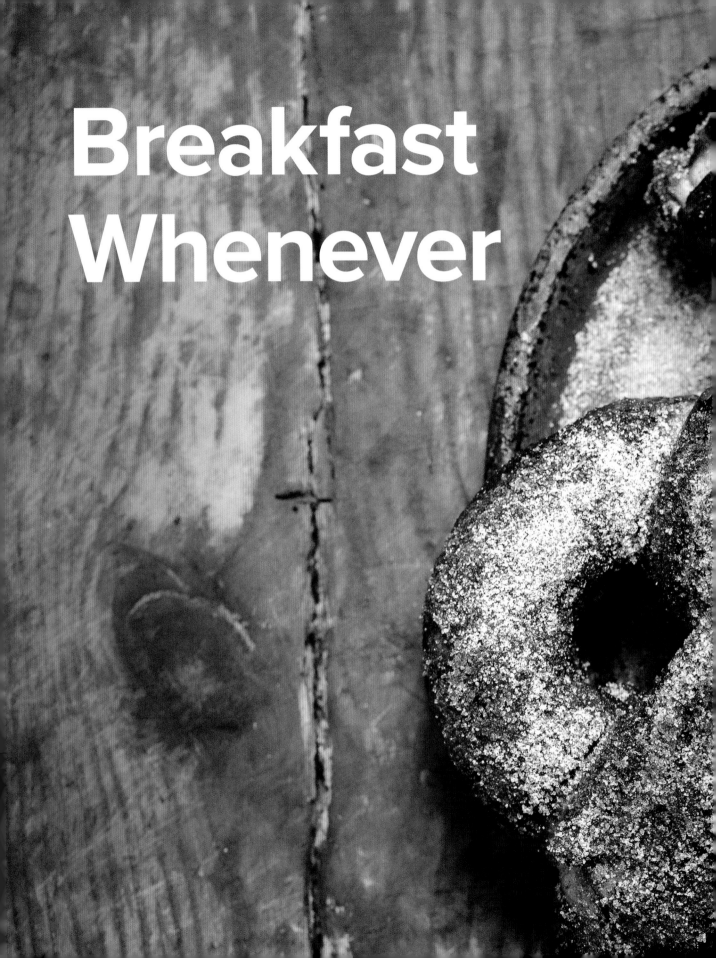

Breakfast Whenever

Citrus Crunch Doughnuts

Let's start by treating ourselves, okay? Warm, freshly made doughnuts are one of the very best things (worth the calories, in my opinion). So, we're going to self-care our way into this book by whipping up some homemade-ish doughnuts that will give any chain or local spot a run for its money. To make doughnuts from scratch, you really need to be in a certain headspace that, for whatever reason, I just can't seem to ever get to. I don't want to do all the things . . . mixing, kneading, rising, frying, etc. But, if I can skip right to the frying part, I'm usually game. Here, we'll give the old-biscuit-can-doughnut-thing a modern makeover with a crazy-good citrus sugar and a creamy 2-ingredient sauce for dunking.

MAKES 6 TO 8 DOUGHNUTS
(DEPENDING ON HOW MANY
BISCUITS YOU HAVE)
APPROXIMATE TIME: < 20 MINUTES

1 cup granulated sugar

Zest of 1 navel orange

**Vegetable or canola oil, for
frying**

**1 (16-ounce) can flaky biscuits
(usually 8 biscuits)**

1 tablespoon lemon curd

⅓ cup sour cream

In a small bowl, mix together the sugar and orange zest. Set aside.

Place a large, deep-sided skillet over medium-high heat, and add oil to a depth of about 1 inch. Line a plate or tray with paper towels.

When the oil is hot enough to cause a small bit of biscuit dough to sizzle immediately, it's ready. Using your thumb, punch a hole through the center of each biscuit and pull it into a ring shape (this doesn't need to be pretty or exact). Working in batches, fry the biscuits for about 2 minutes per side, flipping them when they're very golden brown. Lower the heat if they seem to brown too quickly.

Transfer the cooked doughnuts to the paper towel–lined plate or tray to drain and then toss them right away in the orange sugar, coating them fully.

Combine the lemon curd and sour cream in a bowl and serve alongside the warm doughnuts for dunking.

Blueberries and Cream Sheet Pan French Toast

I may never make French toast any other way, ever again. Simply knowing that it is possible to create a heap of fluffy, golden brown, deliciously flavored French toast without having to stand at a stove, flipping batch after batch, is enough to get me up and at 'em. Not to be confused with French toast casseroles (aren't those basically bread puddings?) this recipe creates perfectly cooked slices of French toast that need only soak in the simplest mixture of blueberry yogurt and eggs to achieve that fetching golden color. Using yogurt helps us knock out three ingredients in one fell swoop—the creamy dairy, a hint of sweetness, and the added bonus of blueberries. But you should use any flavor of yogurt you like. Peaches and cream French toast has such a nice ring to it as well. Strawberries and cream? Also yes.

MAKES 8 SLICES
APPROXIMATE TIME: 45 MINUTES

2 tablespoons butter, melted

3 eggs

2 (5-ounce) containers blueberry yogurt (Greek or regular)

Zest of 1 lemon

8 slices brioche bread (pre-sliced is typically available)

⅓ cup sour cream

Juice of ½ lemon

Maple syrup

Serving suggestions: fresh blueberries, turbinado sugar (optional)

Brush or rub the melted butter all over the surface of a large baking sheet.

Crack the eggs into a large baking pan and add the yogurt, lemon zest, and ¼ cup of water. Whisk vigorously until totally combined. Lay all of the bread slices into the yogurty custard, turning them over to fully coat both sides, and let them sit for a while, while you knock out the next few steps.

Adjust the oven rack to the middle position, and preheat to 375 degrees F.

In a small bowl, stir together the sour cream, lemon juice, and a couple teaspoons of maple syrup (this should be to taste). Set aside.

When the oven is ready, place the soaked bread slices on the buttered baking sheet. Bake until very golden brown on top, and cooked; 30 to 35 minutes.

Top with fresh blueberries and sprinkle with turbinado sugar, if using. Serve with the lemony maple cream and extra maple syrup on the side, if you like.

Note: If you have the time, the longer the bread soaks in the yogurt custard, the better. This is true for all French toasting in general. You can absolutely bake the slices right away, but an even better thing to do is get them nice and coated, and then ignore them for at least half an hour, and up to overnight (in the fridge).

Bacon and Sweet Corn Frittata

You could call this a "crustless quiche" and not be wrong. Or, if you're my son, a "gigantic egg bite." It's also not too far from a corn pudding if I'm being totally honest, and it even gives off some corn chowder-esque vibes. But what's in a name, really? Call it whatever you like! But one thing's for sure—this recipe brings a newfound glory to a simple can of cream-style corn. The alluring combination of smoky, salty bacon and sweet, creamy corn is made even better thanks to a little bit of goat cheese and whatever other cheese you see fit to add. I use what I have around . . . cheddar, Gorgonzola, Swiss—it's all good. Same goes for the milk. You can use half-and-half, cream, or even coconut milk. The difference in the end result is negligible, so use what you like. This is a very inclusive, flexible, unstrict sort of frittata, which makes it taste even better, I think.

SERVES 4 (OR A VERY HUNGRY 2)
APPROXIMATE TIME: 50 MINUTES

6 eggs

⅓ cup milk, half-and-half, or cream

1 (14.5-ounce) can cream-style corn

2 ounces goat cheese

½ cup shredded or crumbled cheese, any kind you like

Salt

Freshly ground black pepper

8 slices bacon, cooked and coarsely chopped

Serving suggestion: chopped fresh herbs, any kind you like (optional)

Adjust the oven rack to the middle position, and preheat to 400 degrees F. Brush a small to medium (2- to 3-quart) baking dish with some of the bacon fat from cooking (or just spray or butter it).

Crack the eggs into the baking dish and add the milk, corn, goat cheese, and shredded cheese. Season with salt and pepper and whisk or beat until everything is evenly distributed. Scatter the bacon evenly around the dish.

Bake until puffed, lightly browned, and set in the middle (give the dish a little jiggle to check that); 30 to 35 minutes. Scatter some fresh herbs on top if you feel like it and enjoy.

Note: If your baking dish is especially full, you might want to err on the side of caution and set it on a baking sheet, to catch any potential spillage during baking. Better safe than sorry, you know?

Croque Madame Morning Buns

These are really just egg and cheese biscuits that have shape-shifted a bit. Here, we're demonstrating yet another fantastic way to wield a humble can of biscuit dough, and while you can customize and play around with the flavors, I am somewhat partial to the ham, Gruyère, and egg combination. A play on France's beloved croque madame sandwich, these biscuit cups bake up into handheld versions that are not only easy to enjoy sans silverware, but they're decidedly cleaner all around. Also, I devised a trick to prevent your cups from overflowing with egg whites: I drop a yolk into each cup and then spoon in as much or as little egg white as will fit. If you have whites left over (you will), you can bake them up in their own little muffin cup alongside the buns, and BOOM—you've got an egg white bite here as well.

MAKES 8 BUNS
APPROXIMATE TIME: 40 MINUTES

1 (16-ounce) can flaky biscuits (usually 8 biscuits)

8 thin slices of ham

8 eggs

½ cup shredded Gruyère or Swiss cheese, plus more as needed

Salt

Freshly ground black pepper

Serving suggestions: Dijon mustard and mayonnaise (optional)

Adjust the oven rack to the middle position, and preheat to 375 degrees F.

Stretch the biscuits out a bit and press each one into its own muffin cup, covering the bottoms and working them up the sides as well, creating "cups."

Put a slice of ham in each cup. Keeping the whites in a bowl as you crack them, gently place an egg yolk into each cup, taking care not to break them. Whisk or stir the egg whites and spoon some into each cup, using as much as will fit without spilling over.

Bake for 20 minutes. Top each bun with the cheese, season with salt and pepper, and bake for 5 to 10 minutes more, until golden and puffed. Let them cool for a few minutes before gently removing them from the pan.

Serve these with punchy Dijon mustard or a Dijon/mayo combo for slathering and spreading, if you like.

Buttery Cinnamon Toasted Remnant Cereal

This recipe sort of bridges the gap between breakfast, dessert, and snacking. Highly congenial in nature, it fits in just about anywhere. But this is the kind of recipe that will, inevitably, be ridiculed by someone, somewhere. **"Cereal!?** *Give me a break,"* they'll say, as their fingers type the same words into a scathing online review. All bridges have their trolls though, don't they? Alas, I'm sharing it all the same, as the idea was given to me by a friend and is simply a torch that must be passed. My dear high school friend, Salli, and I used to fill massive mixing bowls with cereal, using whatever was left of the myriad varieties my family always had around—the remnants. We delighted in each and every colorful combination, snacking on them like bowls of popcorn while we watched Brat Pack movies. This recipe lives in that tradition, to be sure. But in the spirit of cinnamon toast, we're going to fry the cereal up in browned butter, spice it with a shower of cinnamon sugar, and enjoy it warm in a bowl of cold milk.

MAKES 2 SERVINGS

APPROXIMATE TIME: < 10 MINUTES

4 tablespoons butter (salted or unsalted, either is great)

2 teaspoons neutral-flavored cooking oil

3 heaping cups of any unsweetened cereal you like (corn flakes, crispy rice, any manner of Chex, etc.)

½ teaspoon ground cinnamon

1 teaspoon granulated sugar

Serving suggestion: milk

Melt the butter in a large skillet over medium heat. Allow the butter to continue cooking for a minute or two until it just starts to brown slightly—you'll smell the difference. Add the oil and reduce the heat to medium-low.

Add the cereal and cinnamon and allow the cereal to toast in the butter (you can add more butter if you want), stirring often, for 3 to 5 minutes. When it's looking lightly browned and toasty, turn off the heat and add the sugar, stirring to coat.

Immediately spoon the mixture into bowls, add as much milk as you like and enjoy right away, while it's still warm.

Eggs in Potato Purgatory

I am actively having to hold myself back from filling this entire breakfast chapter with nothing but egg recipes—I just love them so. This one, however, currently has my heart. To make a (very) fast version of this Italian classic, we'll use pre-roasted potatoes to save tons of time, and we'll doctor up a jar of marinara sauce, adding creamy butter, punchy shallots, a bit of chicken or veggie stock concentrate and a whole mess of garlic to add amazing flavor. You can make it spicy or not, but just know that if you pass on the chiles your eggs will not be so much in "purgatory," as they will just be in a garlicky, tomatoey bath with a bunch of potatoes. Still a very nice place to be, all told.

SERVES 2 TO 4

APPROXIMATE TIME: 30 MINUTES

2 tablespoons olive oil

24 ounces store-bought roasted potatoes (see Note)

2 shallots, thinly sliced

Salt

Freshly ground black pepper

6 tablespoons butter

3 garlic cloves, thinly sliced

1 teaspoon chicken or vegetable stock concentrate (I like Better Than Bouillon)

1 (24-ounce) jar marinara (garlic and herb/basil, if you can find it)

1 to 2 tablespoons finely chopped Calabrian chiles or 1 to 2 teaspoons crushed red chili flakes

4 eggs

Serving suggestions: chopped fresh green herbs such as basil, dill, or parsley, crusty bread

Adjust the rack to the top third of the oven, and preheat to 400 degrees F.

Heat the oil in a large ovenproof skillet over medium-high heat. When it's shimmering hot, add the potatoes and shallots, season to taste with salt and pepper, and cook until they've picked up some nice golden color and are warmed through, 5 to 6 minutes.

Reduce the heat to medium-low and add the butter, garlic, and stock concentrate to the pan. Cook for 1 minute. Add the marinara and chiles and season a little more, if needed. Let it all simmer for 8 to 10 minutes (a splatter screen or lid is a nice idea here).

Using a large spoon, create "wells" in the sauce and crack an egg into each one. Place the pan in the oven and bake just until the whites are set, 6 to 8 minutes. Top with fresh herbs and serve with bread alongside for dipping.

Note: Almost every grocery store carries pre-roasted potatoes in one form or another, and almost any will do here. I prefer halved roasted red potatoes, but feel free to use any pre-roasted potato that you like. I always get mine in the refrigerated foods section, but you can typically find some in the deli/prepared food section or the frozen food section.

Pumpkin Patch Muffins with Salted Honey Butter

This recipe starts off pretty awkwardly, to be honest. It feels like it isn't going to work out—since the batter is literally just two ingredients. But just trust it. I tend to be a hoarder of pumpkin in the fall, never quite remembering how much I have at any given time, so the cans pile up. These muffins were born from a mildly desperate attempt to use them, and ever since, our mornings have been all the better for it. The key is showering the tops with crunchy, sparkling turbinado sugar, which gives these muffins an addictive texture and makes them look almost bakery-esque. The honey butter is good on anything, honestly, but the sweet-and-salty note it adds to these warmly spiced muffins really makes them feel extra special.

MAKES 9 MUFFINS

APPROXIMATE TIME: 35 TO 40 MINUTES

1 (14.5-ounce) can unsweetened pumpkin

1 (15.25-ounce) box spice cake mix

2 tablespoons turbinado sugar

4 tablespoons salted butter, at room temperature (or you can season unsalted butter with a pinch of salt)

1 to 2 teaspoons honey

½ teaspoon ground cinnamon

Adjust the oven rack to the middle position and preheat to 350 degrees F. Using either a 12-cup muffin pan or 2 (6-cup) pans, grease 9 cups or fit with paper liners.

In a large bowl, stir together the pumpkin, cake mix, and ⅓ cup of water. Gently mix until well blended. Fill the muffin cups to the top with the batter, smoothing them as best you can. Sprinkle each with turbinado sugar. Bake until the centers are done (test with a knife or toothpick), 28 to 30 minutes.

Meanwhile, in a small bowl, stir together the butter, 1 teaspoon of honey, and cinnamon. Add another teaspoon of honey if you want it sweeter. Serve this spiced, salty honey butter with the warm muffins.

Cinnamon-Spiced Dutch Baby Babies with Maple Cream

This is a slightly gussied-up version of one of the most popular recipes I've ever shared on my recipe site, *My Kitchen Little*, and like many of my favorite recipes, it walks the lines between several different things. You could call these sweet Yorkshire Puddings and be close to correct. Or, popovers. But they're not made in a popover pan and they don't quite puff up enough to warrant such a name, so I call them what they most resemble—Dutch baby babies. Clearly this is the move, right? Anyway, I tend to adore anything with cinnamon and sugar, and the drizzle of maple-sweetened cream cheese over the top really sends these babies into a sort of cinnamon roll territory. But again, what's in a name, really?

MAKES 12 BABIES

APPROXIMATE TIME: 45 MINUTES

12 teaspoons plus 1 tablespoon butter

3 eggs

2 teaspoons vanilla extract

1½ cups warm milk (see Note)

1½ cups all-purpose flour

¾ teaspoon ground cinnamon

¼ teaspoon salt

4 ounces cream cheese, at room temperature

1 to 2 tablespoons maple syrup

Preheat the oven to 450 degrees F. Adjust the rack to the middle position. Place 1 teaspoon of butter in each of 12 muffin cups. Set aside.

Combine the eggs, vanilla, and warm milk in a blender. Melt the remaining 1 tablespoon of butter and add it to the blender. Blend until the mixture is frothy and well-mixed. Add the flour, cinnamon, and salt, and blend just until combined.

Place the muffin pan in the oven until the butter melts, 20 to 30 seconds. Take it out as soon as that happens and carefully brush or roll the butter around the cups to grease them fully.

Pour the batter into the muffin cups, filling them a little more than ¾ full. Bake for 15 to 17 minutes, or until puffed and golden brown. Take them out and allow them to cool for 6 to 8 minutes before transferring them to a cooling rack.

Meanwhile, combine the cream cheese and 1 tablespoon of maple syrup in a bowl and add a little bit of water (or milk) until you achieve a smooth, drizzling consistency. If you like it sweeter, add another 1 tablespoon of maple syrup.

Let the Dutch babies cool for a few minutes before generously drizzling them with the cream.

Note: One tablespoon of butter is 3 teaspoons. To warm the milk, microwave it for 20 seconds.

Maple-Sriracha Chicken and Cornbread Waffles

Sometimes the trick to really mastering the "art" of homemade-ish cooking is discerning which elements of a dish are worth making yourself and which parts are already great and have been done for you by your store. This recipe is my attempt to exemplify that truth. Most grocery stores sell fried chicken, and it's usually really good. So, we're going to simply jazz up some store-bought fried chicken by serving it atop some fluffy waffles that we'll make from a box of cornbread mix. The sauce should come with a warning—it's pretty addicting. The creamy blend of spicy sriracha, salty soy sauce, and sweet maple syrup ties the whole dish together. My kids are offered chicken and waffles once a week for lunch at their school, and it's a dish that has risen through the ranks of all-time favorites in our house. This recipe is my compromise, a highly doable way to serve it at home that takes very little time and effort to pull off. Win-win.

SERVES 4

APPROXIMATE TIME: < 35 MINUTES

8 pieces of fried chicken, light and dark meat, or 8 to 12 boneless tenders, at room temperature

1 (8.5-ounce) box corn muffin mix

1 egg

¾ cup buttermilk

5 tablespoons melted butter

1 cup mayonnaise

1½ tablespoons sriracha

1 tablespoon maple syrup

3 teaspoons soy sauce

Serving suggestions: 2 cups Simple Arugula Salad (page 86) or plain arugula

Preheat the oven to 170 degrees F. Adjust the rack to the middle position.

Place the chicken on a baking sheet and put it in the oven to warm it up while you make the sauce and the waffles (if your chicken is cold from the refrigerator to start with, you will need to increase the temperature to 325 degrees F and let the chicken warm up for about 12 to 15 minutes).

Preheat a waffle iron, and grease it with a little melted butter, oil, or nonstick spray. In a medium bowl, stir together the corn muffin mix, egg, buttermilk, and melted butter. Allotting a heaping ¼ cup per waffle, ladle the batter onto the waffle iron and cook according to your manufacturer's instructions, until golden brown, and transfer to a plate or tray. You should get about 6 waffles, depending on how large you like them. You can hold them in the warm oven while you make the rest, if you like.

In a bowl, combine the mayo, sriracha, maple syrup, and soy sauce. Taste and adjust the flavors to suit your preference; there are no rules here.

Serve the fried chicken over the waffles, drizzled with the sauce, and topped with some Simple Arugula Salad.

Chili Crisp Toasted Egg Rangoon Bagels

A mashup of crab rangoon (sans the frying part) and lox and bagels, this recipe is built with ease and flexibility in mind. Seeing as how the word, "imitation" is rarely attached to anything positive, let's go ahead and address the elephant in the room. Yes, we're using imitation crab here, and I'll tell you why. It's typically what is used in crab rangoon, so there's that. But also, fresh crab requires cooking and is quite pricey, and really shouldn't be mixed with a bunch of rich cream cheese. So, this is maybe the one time the imitation stuff is actually the better and smarter choice. I like to mix the "crab" into the cream cheese and then pile some smoked salmon on top. Alternatively, you can skip the crab entirely and stir in some chopped boiled egg, creating more of an "egg salad rangoon" situation. When you introduce a salty, chili crisp fried egg and some peppery arugula into the scene, you've got a flavorful, luxe-seeming sandwich that I may or may not have actually dreamed about.

MAKES 4 SANDWICHES

APPROXIMATE TIME: < 25 MINUTES

8 ounces chive and onion cream cheese, at room temperature

4 to 6 ounces flake-style imitation crab or canned tuna

1 to 2 tablespoons chili crisp (see Note)

2 teaspoons neutral cooking oil, plus more as needed (such as canola or vegetable)

4 eggs

4 plain bagels, split

4 ounces smoked salmon (optional, but delicious)

Simple Arugula Salad (page 86) or plain arugula

Combine the cream cheese and imitation crab, using as much of the "crab" as you like. Set aside.

Spoon about 1 tablespoon of the chili crisp and the cooking oil into a large nonstick skillet over medium heat, ensuring that the bottom is nicely coated with oil. When the oil is shimmering hot, fry 2 eggs at a time, cooking them to your preference. Transfer the cooked eggs to a plate.

Add a little more chili crisp to the pan (about 1 teaspoon), and cook the bagels in the hot, spicy oil until very golden brown and toasted on both sides. Add more chili crisp and oil and repeat until all the bagels are toasted.

Smear some of the crab mixture onto the 4 toasted bagel bottoms and top with some smoked salmon, if using, and a fried egg. Pile some arugula salad on top. Serve with the bagel tops off to the side so as to not crush your masterpiece.

Note: Chili crisp is a Chinese condiment that features garlicky fried chili flakes suspended in oil (along with a few other ingredients). It adds tremendous flavor, texture, and heat to everything, so it's an essential in my kitchen. That said, if you don't care to purchase it or don't like spicy things, no worries. You can sub a little bit of chili garlic sauce or "everything bagel" seasoning, ½ to 1 teaspoon per egg here. A dusting of Old Bay is a great spice for this recipe as well.

Mall Pretzels

While soft pretzels might seem an odd addition to a breakfast chapter, to me they are perfect (*Love Actually* reference). These feel breakfasty to me in the same way a cinnamon roll or cinnamon toast does, so here we are. Homemade pretzels, while delicious and undeniably fun, fall into the "labor of love" category of cooking, and therefore tend to show up in my kitchen very rarely. Store-bought pizza dough gets a *Homemade-ish* twist (ha!) when rolled and shaped into pretzel knots. We'll boil them in a steamy baking soda bath before they enter the oven. This one-minute step is remarkable in its effect on this (and any) dough, and it's amazing how that quick trip through the alkalized water transforms the overall flavor. This is a method you can use in many different ways . . . you can do this to canned biscuits and serve them with the beer cheese on page 133. Or, try pretzeled crescent rolls topped with melted garlic butter and some crunchy salt. I've also done this to canned cinnamon rolls for a fun, Bavarian-esque twist.

MAKES 4 LARGE PRETZELS

APPROXIMATE TIME: 45 TO 55 MINUTES (MOSTLY HANDS-OFF)

2 (16-ounce) balls prepared pizza dough or 2 (13.8-ounce) cans dough (see Note)

2 tablespoons baking soda

1 egg, beaten

¾ cup granulated sugar

1 teaspoon cinnamon

4 tablespoons butter, melted

Note: This recipe works well with any store-bought, prepared pizza dough, whether it's from a can or in a ball or a pre-rolled dough—all will work just fine, though your pretzels will vary a bit in size and maybe total baking time.

Adjust the oven rack to the middle position, and preheat to 350 degrees F. Lightly grease or spray a large baking sheet with nonstick spray.

Place a ball of dough onto a clean work surface and cut it in half. Working with one half at a time, roll the dough into a log that is at least 12 inches in length (the longer they are the easier they are to work with). Shape the log into a "U" and then cross one side (arm) over the other. Lastly, pull each arm back over the pretzel and press or pinch it into the dough, securing it in place. Repeat with the remaining dough, making a total of 4 pretzels. (You could also skip the twisting and make big soft pretzel rods, if you like.)

Combine the baking soda and 6 cups of water in a large pot and bring it to a boil over medium-high heat.

Working in batches if needed, boil the pretzels for about 1 minute, flipping each one carefully halfway through. Using a big, slotted spoon, transfer the pretzels to the prepared baking sheet. Brush the tops and the sides of each with some of the beaten egg.

Bake for about 30 minutes, or until deeply golden brown and cooked through (no doughy pretzels!). If they get too dark too fast, you can place a piece of foil loosely over top. Total cook time will vary depending on the size and brand of your dough.

In a wide shallow bowl, combine the sugar and cinnamon and mix well.

Brush the tops of the warm pretzels with lots of melted butter and shower with or dredge through the cinnamon sugar. These are best enjoyed warm, with a cup of coffee.

Dips
and
Snack
Bowls

THE Dip

(Cheesy Corn and Pickled Pepper Dip)

I don't think I could ever write a cookbook that didn't have at least one dip recipe. It'd be inauthentic of me to do so and thus, here we are—a book with almost too many dips. But this one is **the** one. She's trouble in the best way if you know what I mean. The cast of characters reads a little odd, albeit, but trust me when I say that this stuff is to-die-for great. The sweetness of the corn plays so well with the tangy peppers, and is all held together by a mess of creamy, cheesy goodness that is honestly better than it ought to be. I like it best served right away, but it can also be baked and served warm. If you find yourself making and then eating nothing but this dip for dinner, just know that no one will judge you here. Because well, see the title . . .

MAKES ABOUT 2 CUPS; SERVES 4 TO 6
  AS AN APPETIZER
APPROXIMATE TIME: 10 MINUTES

8 ounces shredded sharp cheddar cheese

¾ cup mayonnaise

4 ounces cream cheese, at room temperature

1 (15-ounce) can Southwestern corn, drained

½ cup chopped mild banana pepper rings

¼ cup chopped pickled jalapeño pepper rings, plus more if desired

3 scallions, chopped, both white and green parts

Serving suggestion: tortilla chips

In a large bowl, combine the cheddar cheese, mayo, cream cheese, corn, banana pepper, jalapeño, and scallions and mix until well blended. Transfer to a serving vessel. Serve with tortilla chips alongside for dipping.

PS If you want to serve this warm (it's great warm), you can transfer the mixture into an ovenproof dish and bake at 400 degrees F until golden and bubbly, about 20 minutes. Just be sure to let it cool for at least 10 minutes before digging in.

Note: Pickled peppers are perfect for adding acid and/or heat to everything from salads and pizzas to tacos and stews. In fact, they're the stars of my favorite Giardiniera Roasted Pork Sandwich Skillet (page 155).

Spice Rack Whipped Cheeses with Hot Honey

The ringer. The secret weapon. The belle of the ball. The one that is always asked to dance first—this is the GOAT. Pun was initially unintended, though there is goat cheese going on here. Anyway, I've been making and sharing versions of this recipe for years, and it truly never gets old. It's so easy and fast to (literally) whip up, that it's a bit of a head-scratcher when you dig in. *Whoa, this stuff is even better than I expected.* I play around with the basic construction of the recipe all the time, but here I wanted to share the way I like to serve it most often—the way that is not only the most hypnotically beautiful to look at, but it also happens to help clear out the spice drawer all at once. Like the perfect black dress, this recipe can be a canvas for whatever extra bits you care to add. There are no real rules here. People fawn over this one—they ooh and ahh with each bite. *What, this old thing?* I simply say. It can't help itself that way.

MAKES ABOUT 1½ CUPS; SERVES 4 TO
 6 AS AN APPETIZER
APPROXIMATE TIME: 5 MINUTES

1 (8-ounce) block feta cheese

4 ounces goat cheese

¼ cup store-bought hot honey, plus more as needed

Topping suggestions: poppy seeds, dried herbs such as oregano, fresh chives, toasted sesame seeds, black pepper, freshly chopped parsley, sweet or smoked paprika, ancho chili powder

Serving suggestion: pita chips

Combine the feta and goat cheese in a food processor and process until totally smooth. You can add 1 to 2 tablespoons of water to help smooth things out, if needed.

Pile the whipped cheeses into a bowl or onto a plate. Make a shallow well in the center and pour the hot honey all over it. Top with whatever dried, fresh, and crunchy things you like or need to use up. Pictured here is a combination of poppy seeds, paprika, chives, and oregano.

Serve with pita chips, for dipping.

Barbecue Chicken Skillet Dip

We love "breakfast for dinner," yes? Yes. But with this dip, we'll entertain yet another joy-driven dinnertime sub-set: "Dip for Dinner." That said, Buffalo chicken dip has really enjoyed quite the ride, hasn't it? Its time in the limelight seems to stretch on and on, with no signs of slowing. But I'm here to tell you that all of our parties, sporting events, and dip-forward occasions will be better for this simple flavor change. I didn't invent this stuff, but I have tinkered with the concept a fair amount and feel this recipe can hold its own amongst the sea of ubiquitous Buffalo chicken dips. Store-bought barbecue sauce and a rotisserie chicken are the hero ingredients here, bringing a happy shot of efficiency to things. But since store-bought sauces tend to be a little sweeter than I love, we'll temper that with some salty soy sauce, ample garlic powder (yes, powder), and a heap of smoky cheddar.

SERVES 6 TO 8

APPROXIMATE TIME: 45 TO 50 MINUTES

2 tablespoons olive oil

3 small yellow onions, sliced

1 rotisserie chicken, shredded or chopped

⅓ cup soy sauce

1 cup favorite store-bought barbecue sauce

2 teaspoons garlic powder

8 ounces cream cheese

8 ounces smoked cheddar cheese, shredded (not pre-shredded), divided

Salt

Freshly ground black pepper

1 cup shredded Monterey Jack, fontina, or mozzarella cheese

Serving suggestions: coarsely chopped fresh cilantro and tortilla chips

Adjust the oven rack to the middle position and preheat to 375 degrees F.

Heat the oil in a large ovenproof skillet over medium heat. Add the onions and cook, stirring occasionally, until they're very tender and partially caramelized, 10 to 12 minutes.

Add the chicken to the pan, along with the soy sauce, barbecue sauce, and garlic powder, and stir to mix. Add the cream cheese and half of the smoked cheddar and stir to blend everything together. Season lightly with salt and pepper, as needed.

Top with the remaining smoked cheddar and the Monterey Jack cheeses and bake until golden brown and bubbly, 22 to 25 minutes. Serve hot, topped with cilantro, and add tortilla chips for dipping.

Herby Garlic and Olive Oil Dip

Billy Joel's "Scenes from an Italian Restaurant," inevitably gets stuck in my head when I make this dip. Visions of red and white checkered tablecloths and drippy, candle wax–coated bottles of Chianti dance in my head with every swipe and swoop through this utterly delicious mixture. It takes just a couple of minutes to make, and it tends to steal the show, always.

SERVES 2 TO 4 AS AN APPETIZER
APPROXIMATE TIME: 5 MINUTES

½ cup olive oil

1 tablespoon balsamic vinegar

1 garlic clove, finely minced

1 teaspoon dried oregano

¼ cup grated Parmesan or pecorino cheese

Flaky sea salt

Freshly ground black pepper

Serving suggestion: good bread (I highly suggest the Pizza Dough Focaccia on page 104)

Pour the olive oil onto a small plate (I use a salad plate). Add the vinegar and minced garlic and stir it around to mix it a little bit. Top evenly with the oregano and cheese and season with salt and pepper. Serve with good bread.

Note: If the raw garlic is a little too much for you, you can swap in ¼ teaspoon of garlic powder or even garlic salt instead.

Salsa for Fruit

While I tend to skew toward the salty side when it comes to my snacking, I really do love this oddly great concoction, in all its subtly sweet, smoky glory. So often our fruit platters are accompanied by tubs of gloopy caramel or chocolate sauces, which just doubles down on the sweetness factor. But to me, fruit is sweet enough already and is maybe best supported by something that complements rather than exaggerates that. Enter this relatively complex and just-sweet-enough salsa that goes so well with any manner of fruit (and also cucumbers) that you see fit to use.

MAKES ABOUT 1½ CUPS
APPROXIMATE TIME: < 5 MINUTES

1 (10-ounce) can crushed pineapple, drained

2 chipotle peppers in adobo

½ cup sun-dried tomatoes, drained

Juice of ½ lime

Serving suggestions: sliced fruit (plums, peaches, apples, and watermelon are especially great)

Combine the pineapple, peppers, sun-dried tomatoes, and lime juice in a food processor or blender and blend until totally smooth. Transfer the mixture to a serving bowl and enjoy with your favorite sliced fruits.

Creamed Mozzarella with Honey-Drenched Sun-Dried Tomatoes

Any recipe that can be described as "pizza adjacent" is almost always going to be a crowd-pleasing thing. As such, this unique rendering of pizza flavors is one that tends to elicit visible delight from any who make its acquaintance. Creaming fresh, delicately flavored mozzarella with either ricotta or cream cheese and using that as a springboard for all sorts of dippables was something of a revelation for me, a new and intriguing way to wield a cheese that is most often fried or melted. Color me smitten. A little store-bought pesto further escorts us down the pizza road, and sun-dried tomatoes—the sweetly shriveled darlings of the 1990s food world—are given full license to shine here, thanks to a little floral honey. Take another little piece of my heart, why don't you.

SERVES 4 TO 6

APPROXIMATE TIME: 5 MINUTES

12 ounces fresh mozzarella cheese (cut into slices or small pieces for easy blending)

8 ounces ricotta or room temperature cream cheese

2 heaping tablespoons pesto

Salt

1 (8- to 9-ounce) jar of sun-dried tomatoes packed in oil (see Note)

2 to 3 tablespoons honey

Serving suggestions: bagel chips, toasted crostini, breadsticks, assorted crackers, raw zucchini slices

Combine the mozzarella, ricotta, pesto, and 1 tablespoon of water in a blender and blend until smooth and creamy. If you need to add a little more water to get things moving, go for it, but just 1 tablespoon at a time. You only want to add water to help the blender do its thing.

Season with salt to taste and slather the mixture onto a plate or platter. Rinse out the blender.

Combine the sun-dried tomatoes and 2 to 3 tablespoons of the oil in which they were packed (see Note) in the blender. Add the honey and blend until a chunky paste-like mixture forms. Pile this on top of the whipped mozzarella mixture and serve with the dipping vehicle(s) of your choice.

Note: If you can't find sun-dried tomatoes packed in oil, just add a little olive oil to the blender, along with the tomatoes; 1 to 2 tablespoons should do.

Creamy Pickle-Chile Dip

This is a real "choose your own adventure" type of dip. If you love bread-and-butter pickles—you should use those. Are dill pickles more your thing? Then go for it! I enjoy this dip either way, and feel you can't really go wrong, no matter how you shake it.

MAKES ABOUT 1½ CUPS
APPROXIMATE TIME: < 5 MINUTES

8 ounces cream cheese

1 (16-ounce) jar pickles, drained, any flavor you love, plus extra chopped pickles for topping (optional)

1 (4-ounce) can green chiles, drained

⅓ cup pickled jalapeños

Salt

Chopped fresh dill, for topping (optional)

Serving suggestion: potato chips

Combine the cream cheese, pickles, green chiles, and jalapeños in a food processor and mix until smooth. Taste and add salt as needed (sweeter pickles will require a little more salt for balance). Transfer the mixture to a serving bowl, top with chopped pickles and dill, if you like, and enjoy with potato chips (these add a fried pickle element to things).

Snack Bowls

Fish and Chips

One of my favorite local-to-me spots is a small Spanish tapas place, and they offer a bowl of salty, briny odds and ends just like this, "the snack bowl." I've riffed on it myself many times, and find that it's always evolving and shape-shifting a bit, but is never without the fish and chips components so as to not waste this perfectly good punning opportunity. So, that's what I'm sharing with you here. This recipe is as much a conversation starter as it is an appetizer. It's cheeky, amusing, and almost always garners a smile from anyone who gets it without having to be told the name. But also? It's really tasty. Kid-beloved Goldfish crackers grow up real quick when paired with some kettle-cooked potato chips, savory Old Bay seasoning, and the anchovies. That could maybe be optional, as I realize they can be a hard sell. Suit yourself, there. But you just might find you like them more than you think you do.

SERVES 4 TO 6 PEOPLE, OR AS MANY
    AS YOU NEED IT TO
APPROXIMATE TIME: 15 MINUTES

3 tablespoons olive oil

3 or 4 anchovies, coarsely
    chopped

3 garlic cloves, peeled and
    smashed

2 cups Goldfish crackers

½ teaspoon Old Bay seasoning

2 cups kettle-cooked potato
    chips

Heat the oil in a large skillet over medium heat. When it's hot, add the anchovies and garlic cloves and simmer gently until the anchovies sort of melt into the oil, 3 to 4 minutes. Add the Goldfish crackers and the Old Bay seasoning and cook, tossing occasionally, until the fish are looking a little golden and smell toasty, about 5 minutes (you can add a little more oil, if needed). Transfer the garlicky Goldfish crackers to a bowl and add the potato chips, tossing a bit to mix everything together.

This mix is best enjoyed the day it's made.

(Photo on page 55)

It's 4:00 in Paris

I recently found a handwritten letter in my daughter's backpack that was intended for none other than the President of France. In what I assume was a Google-translated (unless she's learned French without me knowing) smattering of concise French paragraphs, Elle asked Emmanuel Macron if he could be so kind as to advise us on how to essentially level up our school lunches. "They get baguettes, Mom!" she said to me, "They get things like hams and cheeses and **croissants**!" Somehow my Elle had received a very romanticized description of the French school lunch and regardless of whether it's totally accurate or not, I was wholly amused by the force with which she took on this cause. I also took the opportunity to talk to her about the notion of "le goûter" or, the French afternoon snack time that is something of a cultural phenomenon and traditionally reserved for children. So, while we haven't heard back from the French President yet, we have enjoyed tinkering with our own French-inspired afternoon snacks. This simple combination of pan-fried radishes and baguette slices with a salty, garlic-and-chive butter is my personal favorite.

SERVES 4 CHILDREN OR GROWN-UPS
AS A SNACK
APPROXIMATE TIME: 15 MINUTES

8 tablespoons butter, at room temperature

2 tablespoons minced chives

1 garlic clove, grated or minced

Salt

Freshly ground black pepper

2 tablespoons olive oil

1 bunch radishes, tops trimmed, halved

1 baguette, thinly sliced

In a small bowl, combine the butter, chives, and garlic and season with salt and pepper; set aside.

Heat the oil in a large skillet over medium heat. When it's hot, add the halved radishes and a handful of the sliced baguette to the pan (no need to measure this, just toast as much bread as you like), season with salt and pepper, and sauté until both the radishes and the bread slices are golden, 7 to 9 minutes. During the last minute or so of cooking, add 1 or 2 tablespoons of the garlic-chive butter to the pan and toss the radishes and croutons, ensuring everything gets coated nicely as it melts.

Serve the toasted radishes and croutons with the garlic-chive butter on the side, and extra un-toasted baguette, for spreading and dipping as you like.

(Fish and Chips, see page 53, and Spain, Darling, see page 56)

Spain, Darling

So, Spanish chorizo is already incredibly delicious. We know this. With its deep-set flavors of garlic, pimentón, and salt, this pork sausage is beloved the world over for good reason. But I've found that by simply crisping it up in a pan with some lovely olive oil and yes, even more smoked paprika and garlic (powder this time), we ratchet up the flavor factor to this near otherworldly place. It's just really great. But the very best part of this simple-seeming snack is the abundance of fresh lemon zest that we'll shower down over that hot spiced sausage. It's a truly delicious little bite, and is happy with whatever other tasty morsels you see fit to nestle alongside them. Manchego cheese, Spanish peanuts, chickpeas, torn bread, and crushed Manzanilla olives are always great, but the (Spanish) sky's the limit. I recommend serving this with some toothpicks, as they're the perfect tool for snagging those sausage pieces (and olives + chickpeas for that matter). Just don't forget that downpour of lemon zest—the more the merrier here.

SERVES 4 TO 6 AS A SNACK OR
    APPETIZER
APPROXIMATE TIME: < 10 MINUTES

**3 tablespoons olive oil, plus
    more as needed**

2 teaspoons smoked paprika

1 teaspoon garlic powder

**8 ounces Spanish chorizo,
    thinly sliced, cooked—not raw
    (see Note on page 187)**

Zest of 3 large lemons

**Serving suggestions: 6 ounces
    Manchego cheese, sliced;
    1 (15-ounce) can chickpeas,
    drained and rinsed; ⅔ cup
    Spanish peanuts; 5 to 6
    ounces Manzanilla olives
    (optional)**

Combine the oil, smoked paprika, and garlic powder in a large skillet over medium heat. When the oil is hot, add the sliced chorizo and fry until browned and crispy, 6 to 8 minutes (you can add a little more oil if needed). Transfer the chorizo to a serving bowl, plate, or platter and shower with the lemon zest.

Serve the warm, lemony sausage with any other Spanish-inspired odds and ends that you love.

(Photo on page 55)

Chex and Balances

This is a mix for those who, like myself, suffer from cravings that can only be met by experiencing the whole of the flavor spectrum in one single bite. Yes, the utterly satisfying juxtaposition of **all the things** just really does it for me sometimes, especially when I'm in an indecisive phase. This snack bowl grew from that place. There really aren't many ingredients needed to achieve the following goal of, ahem: *Sweet! Salty! Smoky! Spicy! Sticky! Crunchy! Chewy! Nutty!* No, we're only going to need a few things to pull this off, and boy do they come through for us here. Bacon is always going to be a heavy lifter, let's be honest. Not only does it lend its salty smokiness to the scene, it also gives us some fatty renderings in which to toss the cereal and dates. That, when mixed with the spicy-sweet honey, donates an element of complexity to things, which is really something I never knew I always wanted in a Chex Mix.

SERVES 4 TO 6 AS A SNACK

APPROXIMATE TIME: 25 MINUTES

12 slices bacon, cut into bite-size pieces (about 1 inch)

Olive oil

1 cup pitted dates, halved

¾ cup Spanish or cocktail peanuts

3 cups Chex cereal, any variety

½ teaspoon garlic powder

3 tablespoons hot honey

Salt

Line a plate with paper towels.

Cook the bacon in a large, deep skillet over medium heat until browned and crispy. Transfer the bacon to the paper towel-lined plate and leave the drippings behind.

Add enough olive oil to the skillet that the combination of drippings and oil cover the bottom of the pan. Add the dates, peanuts, Chex, garlic powder, the hot honey, and some salt to the pan and reduce the heat to medium-low. Cook, stirring occasionally, until the cereal is lightly toasted, 6 to 8 minutes.

This will keep, covered, at room temperature for a day or two (if it lasts that long).

Bowl and Spoon

Coconut Curried Sweet Potato and Lentil Soup

SERVES 4

APPROXIMATE TIME: < 20 MINUTES

2 tablespoons olive oil

1 small-to-medium yellow onion, diced

2 sweet potatoes, diced (no need to peel)

1 teaspoon garlic powder

2 teaspoons curry powder

½ teaspoon ground cinnamon

1 teaspoon salt

2 teaspoons vegetable stock concentrate (I like Better Than Bouillon)

5 ounces fresh baby spinach

2 (15- to 17-ounce) cans lentil soup (any variety you like will work)

1 (15-ounce) can full-fat coconut milk

Serving Suggestion: plain Greek yogurt or sour cream, chopped cilantro or scallions, thinly sliced carrot curls, warmed naan

Lentils don't receive nearly as much buzz as they should—at least not in typical American home-cooking chatter (vegan chatter notwithstanding). I just don't see them cropping up in a lot of my family and friends' dinnertime rotations. Here I'm hoping to change that a little bit, seeing as how I'm a true fan of these big/little pulses. In this case though, rather than cooking them from their dried state, we're going to use some good-quality lentil soup as the springboard for a homemade-ish soup that is so fresh and flavorful, people will never guess that it's riding on the humble coattails of a can. The additions of fresh aromatics, quick-cooking greens, earthy curry powder, and hearty sweet potatoes will truly help that can live its very best life. So, the next time you walk past the lentil soup in your store, sitting there playing second (or third!) fiddle to the likes of chicken noodle and tomato, here's hoping you'll be inclined to snag a few cans to use as the supportive backbone in cozy, hearty soups like this one.

Heat the oil in a large pot over medium heat. When it's shimmering hot, add the onion, sweet potatoes, garlic powder, curry powder, cinnamon, and salt. Sauté for 5 minutes.

Add the stock concentrate and spinach and cook, scraping up the browning bits, until the spinach is totally wilted, a couple of minutes. Add the soup, coconut milk, and about 1 cup of water (or as much or as little as you like). Stir to blend and heat. Taste and adjust for seasoning.

Serve topped with plain Greek yogurt or sour cream, chopped cilantro, carrot curls, and warmed, buttered naan on the side for dipping.

Butternut Squash and Pear Soup with Miso Browned Butter

Frozen squash is such a hero item to me. Particularly when employed by a pot of comforting, creamy soup such as this gem. Between you and me, I have injured myself more than once trying to cut a butternut squash, and the time they take to break down and tenderize is really unnecessary in recipes like this. Reach for the frozen stuff and pour yourself a glass of wine as you enjoy all of that time and effort you'll save. The sweetness afforded by a whole can of pears (juice and all) is perfect here, and is made even better thanks to some umami-rich miso paste and a good knob of butter. Refreshingly easy to make and boasting restaurant-quality flavor, this soup is destined to help return both the holly and the jolly to our holiday entertaining, or just a casual weeknight dinner.

SERVES 4

APPROXIMATE TIME: 1 HOUR (MOSTLY HANDS-OFF)

30 ounces frozen cubed butternut squash, thawed and drained

1 small sweet onion, sliced (see Note)

Olive oil, as needed

Salt

Freshly ground black pepper

4 tablespoons butter

1 tablespoon white miso paste

1 (15-ounce) can pears in pear juice

15 ounces vegetable broth

⅔ cup sour cream

2 to 3 tablespoons maple syrup

Serving suggestion: "salad toppers," such as the packs that come with dried cranberries, nuts, and seeds

Adjust the oven rack to the middle position, and preheat to 325 degrees F.

Combine the squash and onion in a baking pan, drizzle with a couple tablespoons of olive oil and sprinkle with salt and pepper. Roast for 45 minutes.

Meanwhile, melt the butter in a medium pot. Once it's fully melted, allow it to continue cooking until small browned bits appear and it smells nutty, 2 to 3 additional minutes.

Add the miso and stir to melt it into the butter. Add the roasted squash and onion along with the pears and juice from the can. Add the broth and, using either an immersion blender or a regular, high-speed blender, purée the soup until it's totally smooth. You can add additional broth or water to thin the soup out further if you like. Taste and adjust for seasoning, adding a little salt and pepper as needed.

Combine the sour cream and maple syrup in a small bowl and serve with the soup along with your salad toppers of choice.

Note: I've noticed that some people get a little panicky when specific amounts of things—like onions—aren't listed in recipes, and I get it. But just know that this is only ever done when exactness isn't required. It's okay if the onion you pick is bigger or smaller than mine. No matter! Each batch of soup gets to be just a little different, but still the same all at once. Like people playing the same song, but in slightly different keys. This is cool. This is the free-spirited nature of home cooking that makes it great. So, don't panic. Just play.

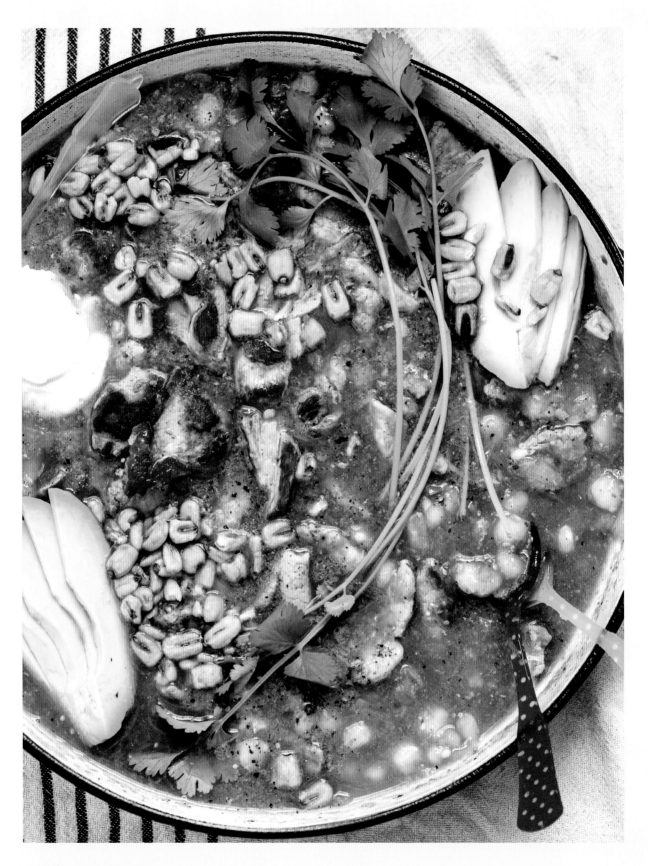

Pork Tenderloin Pozole Verde

A jar of store-bought, verdant, tomatillo-based salsa lends its brightness and incredible flavor to a pot of satisfying pozole. This traditional Mexican stew is built on savory pork and hominy, which are large dried corn kernels that have been alkalized (nixtamalized). Their inherent starchiness gives this stew a rich, almost creamy feel without actually using any cream. As with many soups and stews, this one plays the happy host to a long list of toppings, such as sour cream, fresh herbs, peppery radishes, lime wedges, tortilla chips, and in my corny version (literally), some crushed corn nuts. Just be sure to use low-sodium stock and to season lightly as you go, as the salsa will provide (almost) all the salt that this stew needs.

SERVES 4

APPROXIMATE TIME: 45 TO 50 MINUTES
(ALMOST HALF IS HANDS-OFF)

3 to 4 tablespoons olive oil, divided

1½ pounds pork tenderloin, thinly sliced

Salt

Freshly ground black pepper

1 medium sweet onion, diced

1 teaspoon ground cumin

3 garlic cloves, minced or grated

2 (15-ounce) cans hominy (white or yellow or both), drained

1 (16-ounce) jar salsa verde

3 tablespoons honey

2 cups low-sodium chicken stock

Serving suggestions: chopped cilantro, sliced avocado, sour cream, crushed corn nuts or tortilla chips

Add a couple tablespoons of olive oil to a large deep-sided skillet set over medium-high heat. Working in two batches, add the pork tenderloin pieces to the pan, season lightly with salt and generously with pepper, and cook without disturbing for 5 to 6 minutes, until deeply browned on one side. Toss and stir briefly to lightly sear the other side and transfer to a plate or tray. Set aside.

Reduce the heat to medium-low and add another tablespoon of oil to the pan. Add the onion and cumin and cook for a couple of minutes, until tender.

Add the garlic and cook for about 30 seconds, stirring so it doesn't burn. Add the hominy, salsa verde, honey, and stock and mix well. Add the pork back into the pot, along with any juices. If your pozole needs more liquid, just add water until you get it to the consistency that you like. Allow the stew to simmer, partially covered, for about 20 minutes.

Serve in bowls with cilantro, sliced avocado, sour cream, and crushed corn nuts or tortilla chips, if desired.

Gingery Chicken Noodle Soup with Lemongrass

This incredibly fast and easy chicken noodle soup absolutely takes its cues from its (more mature, more seasoned) cousin, Vietnamese phở. A small nod in that delicious direction, this soup takes the basic structure of a classic chicken noodle soup, and gives it a decidedly Southeast Asian–inspired makeover. The ginger, lemongrass, fish and soy sauces, and unabashedly ample amounts of garlic bring so much interest to an otherwise simple bowl of chicken and noodles. That said, the fact that we're using a rotisserie chicken and some frozen vegetables makes this so very doable on even the busiest of nights. Those nights, incidentally, seem primed to benefit the most from a piping hot bowl of chicken soup.

SERVES 4

APPROXIMATE TIME: 45 MINUTES

1 rotisserie chicken

6 tablespoons cooking oil, whichever you prefer, divided, plus more as needed

1 (10-ounce) bag frozen stir-fry vegetables

Salt

1 bunch scallions, chopped, whites and greens separated

5 garlic cloves, minced

1 tablespoon lemongrass paste (optional)

2 tablespoons ginger paste (or a 2-inch knob of ginger, peeled and minced)

2 teaspoons granulated sugar

2 tablespoons fish sauce

2 tablespoons soy sauce

32 ounces chicken stock

16 ounces rice noodles (or another long noodle), prepared per package directions

Serving suggestions: chopped cilantro

Carefully pull the skin off of the chicken in big pieces, and set those aside. Pull the meat off the bones, and shred it, both the light and dark.

Heat 2 tablespoons of the oil in a large, deep skillet over medium-high heat. When it's shimmering hot, add the frozen vegetables and cook, covered, until they are totally thawed, 6 to 8 minutes. Transfer the vegetables to a plate or tray.

Making sure there's no water in the pan, add 2 more tablespoons of oil. When it's hot, add the chicken skin. Season lightly with salt and cook for about 2 minutes, until golden brown and crisped. Transfer the chicken skin to the tray with the veggies.

Reduce the heat to medium and add another tablespoon or so of oil. Add the scallion whites, garlic, lemongrass paste (if using), ginger paste, and sugar and cook, stirring, for 1 minute. Add the fish sauce and soy sauce and cook, stirring, for 30 more seconds.

Add the shredded chicken and toss to combine. Add the veggies back into the pan along with the stock and reduce the heat to low (everything should be fully submerged; you can add some water if needed). Let the soup simmer, with the lid slightly ajar, for about 10 minutes.

To serve, divide the cooked noodles between serving bowls and ladle in some chicken, veggies, and hot broth. Top with the crispy chicken skin, chopped cilantro, and the scallion greens. This is best served with a spoon for the broth and veggies and a fork for those long noodles.

Tortellini and White Beans in Carrot-Chili Broth

Hailing from Italy's Emilia-Romagna region, there may be no better example of simple, rustic Italian cooking than tortellini en brodo. Classically prepared with handmade meat-and-cheese-filled tortellini and a freshly made broth (classically, hen broth), this dish is pure elegance and is truly more than meets the eye. But in this homemade-ish homage, we'll use good store-bought tortellini and a doctored box of broth to achieve delicious results. The simple addition of creamy white beans, olive oil and butter, dried herbs, and our trick shot ingredient—canned sweet carrots—help to enrich the flavor, fooling our taste buds into believing it simmered all day. But you and I know the truth and let's not tell, okay?

SERVES 4

APPROXIMATE TIME: < 20 MINUTES

1 (15-ounce) can sweet carrots, drained

4 ounces prosciutto

2 tablespoons olive oil

2 tablespoons butter

1 teaspoon chicken stock concentrate (I like Better Than Bouillon)

1½ teaspoons garlic powder

½ teaspoon crushed red chili flakes, plus more as desired

2 teaspoons Italian seasoning

1 (14.5-ounce) can cannellini beans, drained and rinsed

3 to 4 cups chicken broth

20 ounces cheese tortellini (any flavor you like is fine)

Salt

Freshly ground black pepper

Freshly grated or shaved Parmesan cheese

Serving suggestions: chopped parsley, extra-virgin olive oil for drizzling

Adjust the rack to the middle position, and preheat the oven to 400 degrees F.

Purée the carrots in a blender or food processor until totally smooth.

Arrange the prosciutto slices in a single layer on a baking sheet and bake for 8 to 10 minutes, until crisped.

Place a large, deep-sided skillet over medium heat. Add the oil, butter, stock concentrate, garlic powder, chili flakes, and Italian seasoning and cook, stirring, to allow the flavors to "bloom" for a couple of minutes. Add the beans, puréed carrots, and broth and mix well. Season with salt and pepper and simmer over low heat while you cook the tortellini.

Cook the tortellini in salted water according to the package instructions. Drain the tortellini and divide them among serving bowls (using as much per serving as you like) and top with the white beans and broth.

Top each serving with some crispy prosciutto, breaking the slices up into big, jagged pieces. Shower with grated or shaved Parmesan cheese, some chopped parsley, and a drizzle of extra-virgin olive oil, if desired.

Chorizo and Black Bean Chili

SERVES 4

APPROXIMATE TIME: < 15 MINUTES

1 pound bulk Mexican-style chorizo, casings removed, raw—not cooked (see Note on page 187)

1 small onion, chopped

Olive oil

3 garlic cloves, minced

1 teaspoon ground cumin

3 tablespoons chili powder, plus more as needed

2 (15-ounce) cans black beans, drained and rinsed

1 (16-ounce) jar mild chunky salsa

1 to 2 cups low-sodium chicken or vegetable broth

Salt

Freshly ground black pepper

Serving suggestions: sour cream, chopped cilantro, avocado, cut limes for squeezing, warm tortillas or chips

Maybe the easiest chili you will ever make, this one gets its flavor from Mexican-style chorizo, the deliciously spiced sausage that is always worth keeping around for a rainy day. Or, a chilly chili day, for that matter. With only a shallow handful of simple ingredients, this comes together in less than 15 minutes and needs no time to become delicious thanks to the salsa trick. Yes, we'll use a jar of chunky salsa to take care of the tomato portion of the program, along with lots of extra flavor. It just works beautifully here. But, as is the case with just about every stew, soup, or chili, this one only gets better with time, so it's a great make-ahead meal. It will keep nicely in the fridge for up to five days. I like to serve mine with warm flour tortillas or crispy tortilla chips.

Combine the chorizo and chopped onion in a large, deep skillet over medium heat, breaking it up with a spoon to cover as much surface area as possible. (You shouldn't need any oil for this, because the sausage will render enough of its fat, but a drizzle of olive oil is fine if necessary to keep things from sticking). Let the sausage brown without moving it for 5 minutes.

Then, give the chorizo a stir and add the garlic, cumin, and chili powder and cook for another minute. Add the beans, salsa, and broth, stirring to combine. Taste and adjust for seasoning with salt and pepper (it likely won't need much salt). Let the chili simmer over low heat, stirring occasionally, for 5 to 10 minutes.

Enjoy hot topped with sour cream, fresh chopped cilantro, avocados, cut limes for squeezing over the top, and warm tortillas or chips.

Reuben Soup

2 tablespoons olive oil

1 small onion, diced

**24 ounces small yellow
  potatoes, diced**

**2 to 3 smoked sausage links,
  sliced into ¼-inch pieces
  (optional)**

Freshly ground black pepper

2 garlic cloves, minced

**¾ pound thick-sliced corned
  beef, diced**

**¼ cup dill pickle relish or finely
  chopped dill pickles**

**1 (16-ounce) jar sauerkraut,
  drained (about 2 cups)**

¼ cup all-purpose flour

4 cups low-sodium beef stock

**1 teaspoon Worcestershire
  sauce**

½ cup ketchup

**½ cup half-and-half, milk, or
  heavy cream**

**8 slices toasted rye bread,
  cut into bite-size pieces or
  5 ounces seasoned croutons**

8 slices Swiss cheese

**Serving suggestion: chopped
  parsley**

A hearty soup that is inspired by everyone's favorite deli sandwich comes together in a hurry, thanks to the fact that the star ingredient—corned beef—is already cooked. If you also choose to add smoked sausage, that same advantage still applies. So, this is a true chop-and-drop recipe that gets incredible flavor from the likes of sauerkraut, garlic, Worcestershire sauce, ketchup, and pickles (a nod to Thousand Island dressing). Just be sure to use low-sodium stock and to not add any extra salt, as the corned beef adds enough on its own. The addition of creamy potatoes truly rounds this soup out into an ultra-satisfying pot of stick-to-your-ribs fare.

Heat the oil in a large pot over medium-high heat. When it's hot, add the onion, potatoes, and sausage (if using). Season generously with pepper. Cook, stirring occasionally, for 8 to 10 minutes.

Add the garlic, corned beef, pickles, and sauerkraut and mix well. Sprinkle in the flour and cook for 1 minute. Add the stock and Worcestershire sauce, stir, and bring to a boil. Reduce to a simmer over low heat. Add the ketchup and half-and-half and let the soup simmer for about 10 minutes, or until the potatoes are fork-tender.

To serve, preheat the broiler to high and adjust the rack to the top third position. Ladle the soup into individual ovenproof bowls and top with as much toasted rye bread or croutons as you like. Lay a couple slices of cheese over the top and broil for 1 to 1½ minutes, until the cheese is melted and gooey and the bread or croutons are deeply browned. Top each portion with chopped parsley.

Italian Wedding Soup with Roasted Garlic Broth

Canned Italian wedding soup is pretty underwhelming, let's be honest. Scratch-made Italian wedding soup is delicious but somewhat time consuming to prepare. So, here we're going to meet somewhere in the happy middle ground, using store-bought meatballs as a helpful base for a perfectly homemade-ish dish. By only adding a few select ingredients—tons of roasted garlic, for example—we get a pot of soup that not only looks, smells, and tastes great, but that is much more nutritious as well. Just know that it's almost impossible to keep all (even most) of the cheese inside the meatballs as they bake, some is inevitably going to sneak out and this is fine. That cheese will lightly fry in the oven, getting crispy and browned and becoming everyone's favorite part of the whole dish.

SERVES 4

APPROXIMATE TIME: 50 MINUTES

12 uncooked, premade Italian-style meatballs from your grocer's meat department

24 small cheese cubes, any variety you like or can find

40 garlic cloves (pre-peeled garlic is kind of a must here)

3 tablespoons olive oil

2 small onions, diced

1½ cups ditalini pasta

1½ cups pre-shredded carrots

1 teaspoon Italian seasoning

6 ounces fresh baby spinach

6 cups chicken stock

2.5 ounces garlic-and-herb cheese spread, or to taste (such as Boursin or Alouette)

Salt

Freshly ground black pepper

Serving suggestion: grated Parmesan cheese

Adjust the oven rack to the middle position, and preheat to 400 degrees F. Line a large baking sheet with parchment paper.

To create a stuffed meatball, set one on a flat work surface and flatten it with your palm. Place two cheese cubes in the center and then pinch the sides back together, rolling it back into a seamless meatball as best you can, taking care not to over-handle them, as this toughens the meat. Repeat with the remaining meatballs. **Note:** cheese is likely going to sneak out of these during the baking process, which is fine! Because the only thing as good as, if not better than, gooey cheese is crispy pan-fried cheese, which is what you'll get. Win-win.

Arrange the stuffed meatballs on the baking sheet and bake for about 25 minutes, until the meatballs are just cooked and golden brown. Wrap the garlic cloves in a piece of foil, creating a little pouch, and place this directly on the oven rack, roasting for 25 minutes as well.

Meanwhile, heat the oil in a large pot over medium heat. When it's hot, add the onions, ditalini, carrots, and Italian seasoning and sauté for about 5 minutes. Add the spinach and cook until the greens are fully wilted down, a couple minutes more.

Add 4 cups of the stock to the pot. Create a paste of the roasted garlic by mashing it with a fork and add that to the pot. Bring to a boil over high heat and cook, stirring occasionally, until the pasta is done. Add the remaining 2 cups of stock to the pot, along with the cheese spread, stirring to melt and mix it in. Taste and season with salt and pepper as needed.

Divide the meatballs between four serving bowls (along with any crispy, pan-fried cheese that escaped), and top with the hot soup. Serve with grated Parmesan if you like.

Pappa al Pomodoro

This recipe has more homemade-ish trickery going on than just about any other in this book. Store-bought pesto (I'm loyal to Rana brand), store-bought garlic bread, and creamy garlic-and-herb cheese spread make quick work of this classic Tuscan soup. Don't tell my Italian relatives, as this iteration of the beloved bread and tomato soup is certainly a departure from tradition, something that Italians don't take lightly. Thick, hearty, and filled with savory flavor, this soup still manages to come together in no time at all, leaving you with some valuable minutes in your day to do . . . whatever you feel like doing.

SERVES 4
APPROXIMATE TIME: < 15 MINUTES

2 tablespoons olive oil, plus more for finishing

2 (14.5-ounce) cans diced tomatoes with basil, garlic, and oregano (or a 28-ounce can)

¼ cup creamy garlic-and-herb cheese spread (such as Boursin or Alouette)

¼ cup store-bought pesto

1 loaf store-bought garlic bread (from your grocer's bakery, if possible, frozen and thawed also works)

Salt

Freshly ground black pepper

Serving suggestions: freshly torn basil or arugula, Parmesan cheese, olive oil for drizzling

Adjust the oven rack to the middle position and preheat the oven to 400 degrees F.

Heat the olive oil in a large pot or deep skillet set over medium heat. Add the tomatoes, garlic-and-herb cheese spread, and pesto, stirring to help melt the spread and pesto into the tomatoes. Add about 1½ cups of water to the pot and stir. Cover and let it simmer over low heat while you prepare the croutons.

Cut the garlic bread into bite-size croutons, about 1 inch in size. You really only need about 5 cups for this soup, so feel free to save the rest of the bread or leave some uncut to enjoy later. Put the bread on a baking sheet and toast in the oven for 6 to 8 minutes, until golden brown and crunchy. This deep color will act almost like another ingredient, adding flavor to the soup.

Add half of the croutons to the tomatoes and stir to incorporate, sort of smashing them into the soup. Season to taste with salt and lots of pepper. You can add more water as you see fit here. This soup is intended to be **very** thick and hearty. But you can thin it out however you like.

Serve in bowls, topped with the remaining croutons for crunch, a scattering of either fresh basil or arugula, some shaved or grated Parmesan cheese, and a nice drizzle of fruity olive oil.

Creamy Fennel and Tomato Soup

This, the first of two creamy bean-based soup offerings in this book, brings good old canned baked beans to the table in a whole new way. We're going to blend them until creamy and then cut some of their inherent sweetness with the acidity and brightening boosts of both tomato soup and balsamic vinegar. Anise-scented fennel and nutty, salty anchovies make things so much more interesting. One of my favorite scratch tomato soup recipes involves roasting several types of tomatoes with aromatics and brown sugar, and this super quick-fix version honors that recipe to a degree. The brown sugar that is found in most cans of baked beans lends that same sweetness, and makes for a velvety, mellow bowl that is lovely with a dollop of sour cream, and maybe a drizzle of sticky balsamic reduction. If you're only able to find 28-ounce cans of beans, just use half of one and use the rest for Chocolate-Chile Pork Shoulder with Beans (page 163), or you can drain them, rinse them, and warm them on the stovetop with lots of olive oil, garlic, and crunchy salt and serve them on thick-cut, buttery toast.

SERVES 4 TO 6

APPROXIMATE TIME: < 30 MINUTES

3 tablespoons olive oil, plus more as needed

1 small onion, diced

1 bulb fennel, diced (save the frilly green fronds for garnish)

4 anchovies

1 teaspoon garlic powder

Salt

Freshly ground black pepper

2 tablespoons balsamic vinegar

4 tablespoons butter

32 ounces tomato and roasted red pepper soup

1 (16-ounce) can baked beans, drained but not rinsed

Serving suggestions: sour cream, balsamic reduction (see Note)

Heat the oil in a large pot over medium heat. When it's hot, add the onion, fennel, anchovies, and garlic powder and season with salt and pepper. Sauté for 6 to 8 minutes, until tender. Add the vinegar and butter, stir, and cook for 30 seconds more.

Add the soup and the drained beans and simmer for about 5 minutes. Using a handheld immersion blender or a high-speed upright blender, blend the soup until it's totally creamy. Taste and season as you like (I usually add ½ to 1 teaspoon salt and more pepper). Serve with sour cream, a drizzle of balsamic reduction, and some chopped fennel fronds, if you like.

Note: To make a fancy-sounding balsamic reduction, just put about ½ cup of balsamic vinegar in a small saucepan over medium heat. Allow it to gently simmer and reduce for about 10 minutes, until it's about ⅓ the original volume. It will become wonderfully sweet and will thicken into a syrup as it cools, perfect for drizzling over any and every thing.

(Photo on page 78)

Creamy Onion and Butter Bean Soup with Brown Buttered Pretzels

I love canned butter beans. **Love.** Their oversized stature combined with an ultra-creamy texture gives them an inherent coziness that is just perfect for soups. If you can find them pre-seasoned, that's even better. In this very quick and simple recipe, the humble butter bean gets an umami jolt from some miso paste (also made from beans, incidentally). Miso is a true-blue homemade-ish pantry staple, as it elevates just about everything it brushes up against. The addition of luxe crème fraîche gives a subtle tang to the fancy-seeming soup, balancing things out and creating the ideal landing spot for some brown buttered pretzel bits.

MAKES ABOUT 4 (1-CUP) SERVINGS
APPROXIMATE TIME: < 25 MINUTES

3 tablespoons olive oil

3 small sweet onions, sliced

3 (15-ounce) cans seasoned butter beans, drained and rinsed (regular can be subbed, and so can any other white bean you like)

2 tablespoons white miso paste

4 ounces crème fraîche or sour cream

2 to 2½ cups vegetable stock

Salt

Freshly ground black pepper

4 tablespoons butter

1 cup store-bought seasoned pretzels, lightly crushed

Heat the oil in a medium pot over medium heat. When it's hot, add the onions and sauté for about 12 minutes, until tender and lightly caramelized.

Combine the onions, beans, miso, and crème fraîche in a blender and blend until totally smooth (you can add a little of the stock if needed to get things moving). Pour this purée into a medium pot over medium-low heat and add the stock, using as much as you like to achieve your desired consistency. Season with salt and pepper and allow the soup to simmer and heat through, stirring occasionally.

Meanwhile, melt the butter in a skillet over medium heat. Let it continue to sizzle and cook for 2 to 3 minutes, until it's lightly browned and smells nutty. Reduce the heat to low and add the crushed pretzel pieces. Let them gently toast, stirring occasionally, for 4 to 5 minutes.

Serve the warm soup topped with the buttery pretzel pieces.

(Creamy Fennel and Tomato Soup, see page 77)

Salads That Aren't Afterthoughts

Roasted Potato Salad

I've taken this potato salad to many gatherings and never once have I gone without being asked for the recipe. It's delicious stuff, but it's not due to any special genius or trickery of mine. It's the soup mix, all the way. I've only ever used packets of onion soup mix to season and flavor other things—I've never actually made soup out of it—and the happiest use I've found so far is this potato salad. Hands down. Furthermore, using pre-roasted and seasoned potatoes saves so much time, potato salad being a perfect use for them. It's salty and creamy, with bursts of crunch thanks to the celery, and it's amusing to watch as people try to figure out what else is in it, why it's so tasty.

MAKES 4 CUPS
APPROXIMATE TIME: 40 MINUTES

24 to 30 ounces frozen or refrigerated roasted potatoes (seasoned is fine, thawed if frozen)

2 to 3 tablespoons olive oil, or as needed

1 (1-ounce) packet onion soup mix

2 teaspoons paprika

2 celery stalks, thinly sliced

2 to 3 scallions, thinly sliced, both white and green parts

2 tablespoons coarsely chopped dill (optional)

½ to 1 cup mayonnaise, as desired

Salt

Freshly ground black pepper

Adjust the oven rack to the top-third position, preheat to 375 degrees F.

If necessary, cut the potatoes into smaller (½-inch to ¾-inch) pieces if they're particularly large. Place them on a baking sheet, toss with a couple tablespoons of olive oil, and roast for 25 to 30 minutes, until golden brown and very crispy.

Transfer the warm potatoes to a large mixing bowl. Add the onion soup mix, paprika, celery, scallions, and dill (if using). Add enough mayo to fully moisten the salad, using as much or as little as you like (I've learned that people vary wildly on this preference, so I suggest starting with ½ cup and building from there). Mix to fully combine. Adjust anything to suit your taste, seasoning with a little extra salt and pepper if you like (the soup mix is quite salty, so taste first!).

I tend to prefer this at room temperature, but it's nice right out of the fridge as well.

Vinegared Tuna and White Beans with Garlicky "Breadcrumbs"

SERVES 4

APPROXIMATE TIME: 10 MINUTES

1 to 2 shallots, thinly sliced (depending on your preference)

2 (8-ounce) cans tuna packed in oil

2 (14.5-ounce) cans white beans, drained and rinsed (such as butter beans, great northern, navy, or cannellini)

2 to 3 tablespoons vinegar (red wine, white wine, or apple cider vinegar all work)

Salt

Freshly ground black pepper

Olive oil

5 to 6 cups arugula or watercress

Juice of 1 lemon

½ cup sliced almonds, toasted (see Note)

1 cup crushed garlic-and-herb croutons

This salad comes together so quickly it's silly. Truth? You'd have to work pretty hard to screw it up. It's so incredibly flavorful **and** healthy, I find myself making versions of it on the regular. This is a good time to reach for the "fancy" tuna, which is to say, the kind packed in oil. Reason being, it becomes part of the dressing, made complete by a splash of punchy vinegar. Truth again? I love how trendy it's become to shower **everything** with breadcrumbs, and there is no easier way to do it than to simply crush up some flavorful croutons. They're even better this way! Who knew?

Soak the shallots in a small bowl of cold water for 10 minutes prior to using. Drain and pat dry. (This mellows out their bite).

In a large bowl, combine the tuna along with the oil from the cans, the beans, shallots, and vinegar. Taste and season generously with salt and pepper. You can add extra olive oil, if needed.

Scatter some of the arugula on a big platter or on individual plates and toss with some lemon juice and a drizzle of olive oil to taste. Top with the tuna salad, followed by the sliced almonds and as much of the crushed "breadcrumbs" as you like.

Note: To toast the almonds, place them on a small baking sheet and bake in a 350 degree oven until golden brown, 3 to 5 minutes. Alternatively, you can toast them in a dry skillet over medium heat for 3 to 4 minutes, until golden brown and fragrant.

Simple Arugula Salad

My favorite salad is one that is built on only one thing, fresh baby arugula. This, along with the bright punchy tang of lemon juice and the balancing act performed by trusty extra-virgin olive oil, brings so many things to life. It's often the answer to the question of, "what's missing from this dish?" This is something I have around all the time, quite literally. You don't need measurements here, so I'm just going to give you what you do need, and nothing more. Your taste buds can take care of the rest. Just give it all a toss, taste, and adjust as needed.

Fresh baby arugula

Fresh lemon juice

Extra-virgin olive oil

Salt

Freshly ground black pepper

Friendly Herb Salads

Just like the arugula salad above, these herby mixes get along beautifully with just about anything. Nine times out of ten, I'm probably throwing a version of this verdant, flavorful salad or the Simple Arugula Salad (above) on top of my main dishes, as a means of lifting and brightening them. From soups and savory stews to rich braises, broils, and bakes, a finishing burst of fresh green herbs will always make everything just a little bit better. The trick is in knowing that you can and should feel free to use whatever herbs you like. But, if having a jumping-off point is helpful, I'll leave a list of some of my favorite herby combinations that beautifully complement a range of flavors and inspired meals. Everything gets coarsely chopped, drizzled with olive oil and a squeeze of lemon or lime. Season with a little salt and pepper, and your herb salad is good to go.

A good cheat sheet:

Italian dishes: 2 parts Italian parsley + 1 part fresh basil + **1 part fresh oregano**

Mexican or Southwestern-inspired meals: 2 parts parsley + **1 part cilantro** + **1 part scallions**

North African–inspired meals: 2 parts parsley + **1 part cilantro** + **1 part fresh mint**

Mediterranean dishes: 2 parts fresh parsley + **1 part mint** + **1 part dill** + **½ part fresh oregano**

French-influenced meals: 2 parts Italian parsley + **1 part dill** + **1 part tarragon**

Southeast Asian–inspired plates: 2 parts scallions, **1 part cilantro, 1 part basil or Thai basil**

Japanese-inspired recipes: 1 part dried seaweed + **1 part scallions** + **1 part cilantro**

Korean- or Chinese-inspired meals: 1 part scallions + **1 part cilantro** + **1 part green or** red chiles and/or toasted sesame seeds

Jalapeño Cheddar Chicken Salad Sandwiches

This is food doctoring in full effect. Sure, you could season and cook your own chicken and then combine it with the usual chicken salad suspects. That's a delicious thing to do, but it's also fairly time consuming and I remain unconvinced that it's all that necessary. In this version, we're going to take a perfectly fine chicken salad from your grocer's deli (because someone has already taken care of the cooking), and turn it into a better, more exciting version of itself. Regular chicken salad, to me, is just okay. But the easy, blink-and-you'll-miss them additions of spicy, tangy pickled peppers and smoky cheese (plus salt and pepper), lifts that ordinary thing into something extraordinary. All right fine, maybe not *extraordinary*, per se, but it is certainly quite a bit more interesting than it was, and that counts for a lot.

MAKES 2 SANDWICHES

APPROXIMATE TIME: < 10 MINUTES

16 ounces store-bought chicken salad

¼ to ½ cup finely chopped pickled jalapeños

¼ to ½ cup finely chopped mild banana peppers, plus 2 tablespoons of the liquid

½ cup shredded smoked cheddar cheese

Salt

Freshly ground black pepper

2 croissants, lightly toasted and split

Arugula

In a bowl, combine the chicken salad, jalapeños and banana peppers to your taste, the pickling liquid, and cheese and mix well. Season to taste with salt and lots of pepper. Pile this on top of the toasted croissants with some arugula.

Note: If spicy food isn't your thing, try using the zest of one lemon plus its juice, along with some chopped fresh basil and chives, and finely chopped toasted pecans and walnuts for a citrusy, herbaceous chicken salad spin.

Salted Poppyseed, Peach, and Cucumber Salad with Fried Pumpernickel

A splash of sunny fresh lemon juice and a good pinch of both salt and pepper will bring a bottle of poppyseed dressing to life in a big way. When poured all over some crisp, chilled cucumber and juicy-sweet peaches, it's a beautiful thing. But the addition of freshly toasted pumpernickel croutons really makes this salad special, befitting just about any occasion.

SERVES 4

APPROXIMATE TIME: 10 MINUTES

1 to 2 shallots, thinly sliced

⅔ cup poppyseed dressing

Salt

Freshly ground black pepper

Juice of ½ lemon, plus more as needed

4 tablespoons butter

2 tablespoons olive oil, plus more as needed

3 to 4 slices dark pumpernickel bread, torn or cut into bite-size pieces

2 fresh peaches, sliced

1 cup sliced English cucumber

Soak the sliced shallots in a small bowl of ice water for 10 minutes. This lessens their intensity while preserving the oniony bite (a nice trick).

In a bowl, season the poppyseed dressing with salt, pepper, and lemon juice to taste (we're trying to counteract the supersweetness and bring more of a balance to the flavors).

Heat the butter and oil in a large skillet over medium heat. Add the pieces of bread and season with salt and pepper. Cook, stirring occasionally, until the bread is crunchy on the outside. They'll smell toasty when they're ready.

Drain the water from the shallots and pat them dry. Arrange the peaches, cucumber, and shallots on a big platter or on individual plates and drizzle or toss with the dressing. Season lightly with more salt and pepper if you like. Scatter the fried bread all over and serve.

Note: During the colder months, when peaches aren't in season, try swapping in any manner of tree fruit, such as apples, pears, or even persimmons. Sliced or segmented citrus works beautifully as well (grapefruit, blood oranges, etc.).

Chipotle Tortellini Caesar with Crispy Kale

People love to hate on bagged salads, don't they? Not me, though. I'm always throwing one or two in my shopping cart, as I value the time they save me too much to be bothered by any silly salad snobbery. A salad kit is just a nice head start, and they can point you in the direction of something pretty great. This pasta salad leverages a bagged Caesar salad and draws out the very best parts of it. Store-bought Caesar dressing is usually okay, but the addition of some smoky, spicy chipotle peppers transforms it. Be sure to add the remaining seasoned oil from the roasted kale pan into the dressing, too—it's such a great trick. A few other subtle but effective hacks make this bagged salad story anything but boring.

SERVES 4 TO 6

APPROXIMATE TIME: 25 MINUTES

6 cups baby kale leaves

¼ cup olive oil, plus more as needed

Salt

Freshly ground black pepper

1 (10-ounce) bagged Caesar salad kit

1 chipotle pepper, plus 1 teaspoon adobo sauce from the can

½ teaspoon garlic powder

9 ounces cheese tortellini, cooked per package directions

Serving suggestion: shaved Parmesan (optional)

Optional protein add-ons: 1 (4 to 5-ounce) can tuna in oil, drained and flaked or 1 (15-ounce) can white beans, drained and rinsed

Adjust the oven rack to the top position, and preheat to 375 degrees F.

Arrange the kale leaves evenly on a large baking sheet. Coat with the olive oil and season lightly with salt and pepper. Roast for 15 to 20 minutes, or until golden and crispy.

Meanwhile, put the Caesar salad dressing in a small bowl and add the chopped chipotle pepper, garlic powder, and about 2 teaspoons of water. Add any excess oil from the roasted kale pan into the dressing and stir to blend it all together. If you like it extra spicy (like I do), add 1 teaspoon of the adobo sauce from the can.

In a large bowl or on a big platter, toss together the tortellini with the Caesar salad greens. Crush up the croutons, turning them into breadcrumbs, and scatter them over the salad, along with any cheese included in the salad kit.

Add the roasted kale to the salad and shave some fresh Parmesan over top (**so** much better than the stuff in the bag). If using, scatter the flaked tuna or white beans all around.

Serve the spicy, smoky dressing either alongside the salad, or you can dress it before if you prefer.

Remixed Greek Salad with Sun-Dried Tomato Dressing

All right, so. Even in all of its palate-assaulting glory, I find the tanginess of a traditional Greek salad to be totally addicting. It is a craveable thing to be sure. So, finding ways to play with the cast of characters, shuffling them around into new roles, is a thing I enjoy. Here, we'll balance the punchiness of feta with some floral honey and pile the (already) marinated artichokes and olives on top. We will jazz up a store-bought bottle of Greek dressing with some bacon-yes-bacon and some sweet sun-dried tomatoes. With some warm, fluffy pita bread or pita chips on the side for dredging, this makes for a stellar lunch. The addition of white beans or chickpeas, or some shredded rotisserie chicken or flaked tuna will boost the protein count and make this a totally satisfying, well-rounded meal.

SERVES 4

APPROXIMATE TIME: 30 MINUTES

1 cup feta cheese

¼ cup honey

6 or 7 slices center-cut bacon

1 cup julienned sun-dried tomatoes (packed in oil, or not), drained and minced

¾ cup Greek dressing

Salt

Freshly ground black pepper

1 cup pitted marinated olives, any kind you like

1 (12-ounce) jar marinated artichoke hearts

1 pint fresh grape or cherry tomatoes, halved if you want

1 cup sliced English cucumber

1 shallot, thinly sliced

Serving suggestions: warmed pita bread or crunchy pita chips

Line a plate with paper towels.

Combine the feta and honey in a food processor or blender (or you can just whisk them) and process until smooth. Spread this all over a big platter or on individual plates.

Cook the bacon in a large, deep-sided skillet over medium heat, turning as needed, for 8 to 10 minutes, until browned and crispy. Transfer to the paper towel–lined plate and leave the drippings in the pan.

Reduce the heat to low, add the sun-dried tomatoes, and cook for 1 minute. Add the dressing and stir well. Season with salt and pepper to taste.

Top the honeyed feta with the olives, artichoke hearts, cherry tomatoes, cucumber, and shallot. Chop or tear the bacon into bite-size pieces and arrange them all around. Serve with the warm tomatoey bacon dressing and some pita or pita chips on the side.

Note: If you don't plan to serve the salad right away, you can still assemble everything, but don't smear the feta on first. Keep that separate, and serve it on the side, along with the dressing.

Cloud Caprese Cups

This is one of my favorite salads to both serve and eat. I am inordinately amused by the fact that you can whip mozzarella in a food processor, creating this fluffy, cloudlike heap of cheese that is great in, on, and around so many things. That's primarily why I'm sharing this recipe with you, actually. Of all the myriad ways we've enjoyed mozzarella—fried, marinated, baked, skewered, etc.—the whipped version doesn't get a ton of airplay. So I'm shining a light on it here. Plus? It's a great way to get a taste of summer all year long, as cherry tomatoes are seasonally agnostic. They're pretty good all the time. If you're using it, just be sure to grab a good-quality pesto (I like Rana), and you're off to the races.

SERVES 4

APPROXIMATE TIME: < 10 MINUTES

16 ounces fresh mozzarella cheese

½ teaspoon salt, plus more as needed

1 tablespoon pesto (optional)

Freshly ground black pepper

1½ pints cherry or grape tomatoes, halved

1 tablespoon balsamic vinegar

1 tablespoon olive oil

Serving suggestion: fresh basil (optional)

Combine the mozzarella, 2 tablespoons of water, the salt, the pesto (if using), and some pepper in a food processor and process until totally smooth.

Toss the tomatoes in a bowl with the vinegar and olive oil. Season with salt and pepper.

Divide the tomatoes between each of 4 glasses/cups/serving vessels. Top with a big heap of the whipped mozzarella and, if you like, a basil leaf or two.

Roasted Coleslaw with Sweet Feta Dressing

Remember in the 1990s when "deconstructing" foods was all the rage? I'm clearly not over the trend just yet, because that is essentially what we're doing with this recipe. Roasted cabbage is a wonderful thing, and if you've never tried it, you're in for a pleasant surprise. I say that because I'm not sure cabbage is a food that is often met with much excitement, and I'm hoping to change some minds here. These dual-toned wedges are seasoned generously and brushed with a store-bought slaw dressing, the inherent sugar content of which will serve to boost the crunchy caramelization of things. The wedges crisp on their outsides, while the insides collapse into these silken rags of sorts—and I mean that in the best way. We'll whip the rest of the dressing with salty feta cheese and a little squeeze of roasted lemon juice, serving to knock out some of that overly sweet, store-bought flavor. Freshly shaved carrots and a shower of either sesame or poppy seeds finish things off nicely, reexamining the whole concept of coleslaw in a most delicious way.

SERVES 6 TO 8

APPROXIMATE TIME: 1 HOUR (MOSTLY HANDS-OFF)

½ head green cabbage, cut into 4 to 5 wedges (see Note for a great way to use up the other half)

½ head red cabbage, cut into 4 to 5 wedges

About ¼ cup olive oil, for brushing

Salt

Freshly ground black pepper

12 to 15 ounces coleslaw dressing

1 lemon, halved

4 ounces feta cheese

2 carrots, shaved into ribbons with a vegetable peeler

Serving suggestion: toasted sesame seeds or poppy seeds (optional), freshly chopped parsley

Adjust the oven rack to the middle position, and preheat to 375 degrees F. Cover a large baking sheet with aluminum foil (helps hugely with cleanup) and brush or spray it with olive oil or nonstick spray.

Arrange the cabbage wedges on the baking sheet and coat or brush them on all sides with olive oil and season generously with salt and pepper. Brush some of the coleslaw dressing all over the wedges, using about ¼ cup or so in total.

Put the lemon halves on the pan, cut-side down, and roast everything for 45 to 55 minutes, until the cabbage is golden brown and slumped.

Meanwhile, combine the remaining dressing with the feta cheese and a good pinch of salt and some freshly ground pepper.

Squeeze some of the roasted lemon juice into the dressing, to taste, and mix well. Pour the dressing all over a platter or individual plates. Transfer the cabbage wedges to the platter or plates, on top of the dressing, and pile the shaved carrot over top. Shower with toasted sesame seeds or poppy seeds, if you like, and some freshly chopped parsley. Serve with extra dressing drizzled over or on the side.

Note: Need a way to use up the leftover cabbage? Try searing it (either shredded or left in big wedges), in a large skillet with lots of butter, salt and pepper, a few anchovies, and some crushed chili flakes. This makes for a sneaky great side dish that I tend to come back to over and over again.

Blooming Onion Smoked Salmon Salad with Squash Ribbons

A certain infamously addictive fried onion appetizer from one Aussie-inspired chain steakhouse stands as the inspiration behind this fantastic salad. I can't ever seem to get enough smoked salmon—I just love the stuff—and this salad features a big portion of it, all splayed out over a bed of greens with some "ribboned" squash and a shower of crushed french-fried onions (yes, the ones people use on old fashioned green bean casseroles). The dressing is a dupe of the actual sauce you get at the aforementioned restaurant, and the end result is a uniquely delicious salad that makes for a perfect lunch and/or dinner . . . especially when paired with a fresh loaf of Pizza Dough Focaccia (page 104).

SERVES 2 TO 4

APPROXIMATE TIME: < 10 MINUTES

5 cups mixed greens or spring greens

8 to 10 ounces cold smoked salmon

1 zucchini

1 yellow squash

1 cup crushed store-bought french-fried onions

¾ cup mayonnaise

½ cup creamy horseradish

2 tablespoons ketchup

½ teaspoon garlic powder

½ teaspoon smoked paprika

Arrange the greens on a big platter or on individual plates. Tear or cut the salmon into bite-size pieces and lay them across the greens. Using a vegetable peeler, shave the zucchini and yellow squash into long strands. Arrange those on the salad as well, followed by the crushed fried onions.

In a bowl or liquid measuring cup, stir together the mayo, creamy horseradish, ketchup, garlic powder, and smoked paprika. If you prefer a thinner dressing, you can add a splash of water until the consistency is to your liking. Taste and adjust the ingredients to suit your preference.

Serve the salad with the dressing on the side or drizzled over top.

Hard-Roasted Cauliflower with Champagne Gribiche

I'm not sure if this really qualifies as a "salad" per se, but it is a vegetable that is served with a dressing, so we're going to just go ahead and say it does. But really, this recipe works well as a salad, starter, or side dish and plays nicely with most any other characters that you want to add into the scene. Steak? Yes, absolutely. Saucy fish? Sure! Roasted chicken? I don't see why not. The hard-roasting here refers to the fact that we're going to cook the cauliflower at high heat on the floor of the oven (or, the very lowest rack if you can't remove yours). This ensures a truly great charring that is even and consistent every time. Sauce gribiche is a cold French sauce made from eggs, pickles, Dijon mustard, oil, often vinegar, and herbs. Our homemade-ish version will use a bottled champagne vinaigrette and some store-bought boiled eggs as the heavy lifters. It comes together in about a minute and, thanks to the addition of some dill pickles, has a flavor so bright and tangy that it beautifully lifts the more subtle, earthy vibes of the roasted cauliflower.

SERVES 4

APPROXIMATE TIME: 30 MINUTES

2 heads cauliflower

3 tablespoons olive oil, plus more as needed

Salt

Freshly ground black pepper

6 hard-boiled eggs

¼ cup dill pickle slices or chips

¾ cup store-bought champagne vinaigrette

Serving suggestion: toasted sesame seeds, chopped fresh parsley

Remove the lowest oven rack if you can or adjust a rack to the lowest position possible. Preheat the oven to 450 degrees F.

Trim the thick stem and green leaves off the cauliflower and cut each head into bite-size florets of about the same size. How big you make them doesn't matter so much as ensuring the pieces are all roughly the same size (this helps with even cooking).

Transfer the cauliflower florets onto a large baking sheet. Coat the cauliflower evenly with oil and season with salt and pepper. Roast for 10 minutes. Stir and turn the florets and roast in increments of 5 minutes, stirring in between each, until tender and beautifully charred all over. It usually takes me a total of about 20 minutes.

Meanwhile, combine 2 of the eggs, the pickles, and vinaigrette in a food processor and blend until mostly smooth. Add the remaining 4 eggs and pulse just to chunk them up and evenly distribute them throughout the sauce.

Serve the roasted cauliflower either with the gribiche on the side or you can pour some of it on a platter or plates, using it as an anchor for the cauliflower, which can be piled on top. Scatter some toasted sesame seeds and chopped parsley on top.

Pasta, Grains, and Meatless Mains

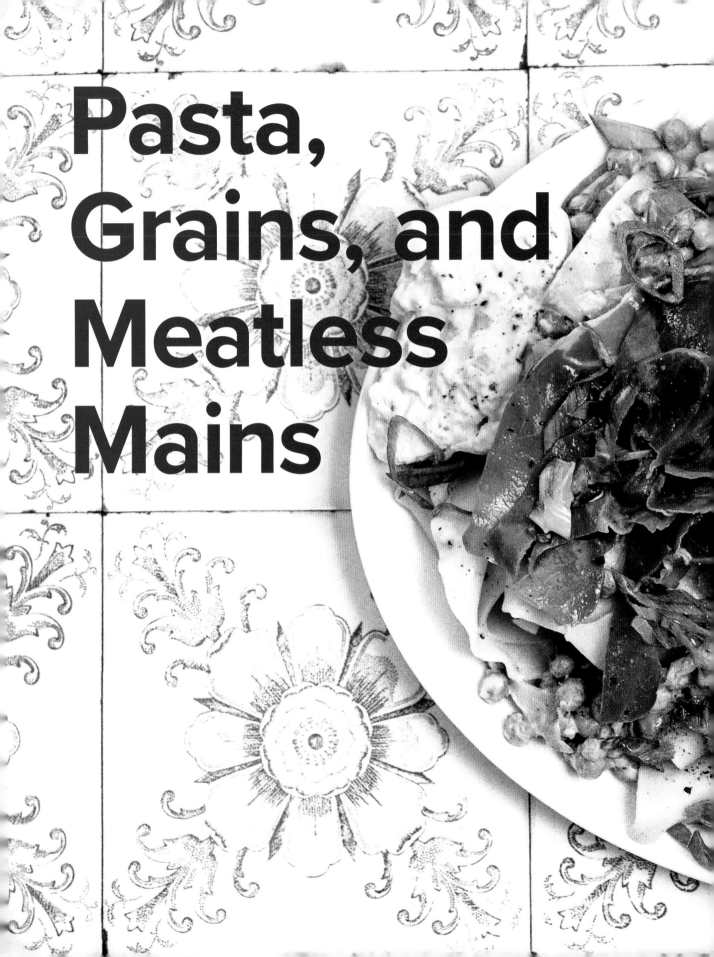

Pizza Dough Focaccia

This recipe was a bit of a game-changer for me, lover of carby, bready things that I am. Now, I love bread baking projects, sure, but mostly I love them in theory. You'll likely never find me baking fresh bread on like, a Wednesday afternoon. But this focaccia? Whole different story. By using some of my best tricks for scratch-made focaccia to elevate a ball of store-bought pizza dough, we can create this incredibly delicious homemade-ish focaccia that is salty and crunchy on the outside and perfectly fluffy and bubbly inside. We'll pour a basic olive oil brine all over the dough that will serve to both flavor the crust and help it to build a fetching golden-brown color. This stuff comes together so fast and simply, you can pull it off any day of the week. Now that's amore.

MAKES 1 (8 X 12-INCH) LOAF (GIVE OR TAKE)

APPROXIMATE TIME: < 1 HOUR (MOSTLY HANDS-OFF)

3½ tablespoons olive oil, divided

1 (16-ounce) ball store-bought pizza dough

½ teaspoon salt

Flaky sea salt, for sprinkling

Freshly ground black pepper

1 tablespoon dried oregano (optional)

Pour 2 tablespoons of the olive oil into a 9 x 13-inch baking pan. Place the dough inside the pan and pat and work the dough into a rectangle that (mostly) fills the pan. Allow it to rise in a warmish place for 30 minutes (Tip: set it in an oven that was warmed on 170 degrees F for a few minutes. Keep the heat off but let the residual warmth help speed up the proofing/rising process.)

Adjust the oven rack to the middle position, and preheat to 425 degrees F.

In a small bowl or liquid measuring cup, whisk together the remaining 1½ tablespoons olive oil, the salt, and 1½ tablespoons of hot water to make a brine.

Using your fingertips, poke deep holes/indentations down into the dough, pockmarking the entire surface. It's not going to be as poofy/thick as homemade dough would be—no matter. Pour the brine all over the surface of the dough (It will seem like a lot, but trust the process!). Sprinkle the dough evenly with flaky sea salt, lots of freshly ground pepper, and the oregano (if using).

Bake for 20 to 24 minutes, until deeply golden on top and done on the bottom as well. If the top gets too dark before the bread is totally done, lay a piece of aluminum foil over top. Drain off any excess oil/brine and transfer the hot bread to a cutting board before cutting into slices and serving warm.

Ballpark Garlic Fries

I'm not sure French fries require much preamble. They're one of the most universally beloved foods, with cultures all over the world claiming their own unique versions. From the crispy, salty frites served alongside steaming mussels on the streets of Brussels, to Lebanese-style *batata maqlieh*, served with a lemony garlic dip called *toum*, and the wild tangle of curlicued fries they serve at Dollywood in Tennessee, I will take them any way I can get them. Here, we're going to dress up some frozen fries Dodger Stadium–style with garlic oil and tons of fresh parsley.

SERVES 4 AS AN APPETIZER OR
  SIDE DISH
APPROXIMATE TIME: 25 MINUTES

28 ounces frozen French fries (preferably skin-on, shoestring style)

⅓ cup vegetable oil

¼ cup olive oil

7 to 8 large garlic cloves, minced

1 teaspoon Italian seasoning

Salt

Freshly ground black pepper

½ cup finely chopped fresh parsley

Preheat the oven to the temperature on the fries' package and prepare them as directed.

Meanwhile, make the garlicky topping. In a saucepan over low heat, combine the oils, garlic, and Italian seasoning. Season lightly with salt and lots of pepper and mix well.

Let the mixture just barely come to a simmer and then turn off the heat. Let this sit while the fries finish baking.

When the fries are done, pour the garlicky oil all over them, right on the baking sheet. Add the parsley and toss, toss, toss to get the fries nice and coated. Season with salt and pepper, if needed. Transfer them to a serving platter and enjoy warm.

Garlic and Herb Bubble Bread

If the name here alone doesn't inspire you to investigate further into what, exactly, this stuff is, I don't know what would. I'm a sucker for a tasty-sounding moniker myself, and the first time I laid eyes on "bubble bread" I was like, oh hello, I don't know exactly what you are but I'm going to be meeting you very soon. Ahem. Anyway, I now know precisely what this stuff is and I'm more than happy to sing its praises here. It's probably best described as a savory monkey bread, and incredibly fast and easy to whip up thanks to canned biscuit dough. It's totally unpretentious and is just very friendly stuff. Family friendly. Kid friendly. Dinner party friendly, Holiday friendly. With-your-morning-eggs friendly. You get the idea.

SERVES 4 TO 6

APPROXIMATE TIME: 35 TO 40 MINUTES

1 (16-ounce) can flaky biscuits

4 tablespoons unsalted butter

3 tablespoons olive oil

1 teaspoon Italian seasoning

3 garlic cloves, minced or grated

Salt

1 cup shredded mozzarella or fontina cheese

Adjust the oven rack to the middle position, and preheat to 350 degrees F.

Cut each biscuit into quarters. Roll each piece into a ball and place them in a 9 or 10-inch baking dish, leaving a little space in between them, as they'll expand or "bubble" up. (You can use any dish you like, from a cake pan or pie plate to a ceramic baking dish or brownie pan. I often use a round pie plate or even a 9 x 13-inch baking dish. This is flexible!)

In a small saucepan over medium-low heat, combine the butter with the olive oil, Italian seasoning, garlic, and a good pinch of salt. Stir to blend. When the butter has just melted, pour the mixture all over the biscuit pieces, and roll them around to coat fully.

Bake for 15 to 17 minutes, or until golden on top. Cover the bread evenly with the cheese and bake for 3 or 4 more minutes, until the cheese is fully melted and is optimally gooey. Serve warm.

Crushed Olive and Date White Pizza with Hot Honey

The thing about homemade pizza is this: there are no rules. By their very nature, homemade pizzas are a playground for creativity and having fun. It's a canvas you get to paint, right? Want to make a vegan pizza on a cauliflower crust? Nice. Feel like trying your hand at a Tex-Mex inspired pizza, or a white clam pizza, or a pizza in the shape of the Millennium Falcon? All good. The point is simply to pizza, because even mediocre pizza is still pretty great. This recipe is here not to tell you how to make the world's best pizza (I'm not an expert; there are entire tomes devoted to this), but to pass along a favorite "grown-up" flavor combo of mine, and as a gentle reminder "to pizza" whenever you can. Sitting down with this North African–inspired one is something of a sacred thing to me, it's my happy space. Spicy, briny, sweet, and funky, each bite is a total experience.

MAKES 1 (12-INCH) PIZZA
APPROXIMATE TIME: 30 MINUTES

2 tablespoons olive oil, plus more as needed

1 (8-ounce) package garlic-and-herb spread (such as Boursin)

1 (16-ounce) ball store-bought pizza dough

1 cup marinated pitted green olives, lightly crushed with your hand (keeps them from rolling and is faster than slicing)

4 or 5 pitted Medjool dates, finely chopped

½ to ⅔ cup crumbled blue cheese (feta is a good sub)

¾ to 1 cup shredded mozzarella

Store-bought hot honey, for drizzling

Fresh basil or arugula for topping (any fresh, green thing you like, really)

Preheat the oven to 450 degrees F. Coat a large baking sheet with a thin layer of olive oil.

Combine the garlic-and-herb spread and 2 tablespoons of olive oil in a small saucepan over medium heat and allow the spread to melt into the oil. Add ¼ cup of water and stir to fully blend.

I usually stretch or work my pizza dough directly on the baking sheet, but you can also do this on a clean, flat surface that has been dusted with flour—it's up to you. Stretch and work your dough into a big pizza that somewhat resembles a rectangle. Just fill the baking sheet, getting it as thin as you can, and call it good.

Leaving at least a ½-inch border (for the crust), brush the pizza with the garlicky creamy "white sauce." Use as much as you like, but you may not need to use it all (leftovers are good for dipping crusts). Top with the olives, dates, and cheeses.

Bake for 18 to 20 minutes, until the crust is deeply golden brown and the pizza is bubbly and cooked (your cook time will depend on the thickness of your crust). Drizzle with as much hot honey as you like, and top with the basil or arugula.

Indian-ish Butter Cauliflower

SERVES 4

APPROXIMATE TIME: 40 MINUTES

1 large head cauliflower, trimmed and cut into small florets (about 1-inch)

1 (14.5-ounce) can chickpeas, drained and rinsed

2 tablespoons olive oil, plus more as needed

6 teaspoons garam masala, divided

2 teaspoons ground cumin, divided

2 teaspoons ground coriander, divided

4 teaspoons chili powder, divided

4 to 5 teaspoons ground turmeric, divided

2 teaspoons salt, plus more as needed

Freshly ground black pepper

3 tablespoons butter, divided

1½-inch piece fresh ginger, peeled and grated or finely chopped

1 (24-ounce) jar marinara

1½ teaspoons granulated sugar

1 (14.5 ounce) can coconut milk

Serving suggestions: chopped cilantro, instant basmati rice, and naan for serving.

While it's simple to make, this is the longest-reading recipe in the book, thanks to the wonderful lineup of spices. Indian cuisine is one of my favorites to explore, and there's nothing like a big pan of richly sauced and spice-roasted *anything* to bring my people to the table. This stuff *beckons*, let me tell you. I shared this time-saving butter sauce hack with an Indian friend of mine and, though he teased me a little, he also gave it a big thumbs-up. The trick here is doctoring up a jar of (already seasoned and cooked) marinara sauce with some classic Indian spices, to kick-start the flavor. Is it a dead ringer for a classic Indian sauce? No, of course not. It's more like a marinara sauce that showed up to a costume party dressed as Indian butter sauce. Obviously, a marinara underneath, but bearing a strong likeness. It's a good time no matter how you shake it.

Adjust the oven rack to the middle position, and preheat to 375 degrees F.

On a large baking sheet, toss together the cauliflower, chickpeas, 2 tablespoons of oil (plus more, if needed to fully coat), 3 teaspoons of garam masala, 1 teaspoon of cumin, 1 teaspoon of coriander, 2 teaspoons of chili powder, 2 teaspoons of turmeric, 1 teaspoon of salt, and lots of freshly ground pepper.

Roast the cauliflower and chickpeas for about 25 minutes, until deeply golden brown.

Meanwhile, heat the butter in a large, deep-sided skillet over medium heat. Add the remaining 3 teaspoons of the garam masala, 1 teaspoon of cumin, 1 teaspoon of coriander, 2 teaspoons of chili powder, 2 to 3 teaspoons of turmeric, 1 teaspoon of salt, and lots of pepper (these are approximate amounts—use as much as you like). Cook, stirring, for 3 to 5 minutes.

Add the ginger and cook for 1 minute. Add the marinara, sugar, and coconut milk, stir to combine, and simmer over low heat for 5 to 7 minutes, until the cauliflower and chickpeas are done.

Taste and adjust for seasoning. Slide the cauliflower and chickpeas into the pan (alternatively you can just pile them on top of the plated rice and sauce, as pictured). Serve with instant (or freshly cooked) basmati rice, naan, and a shower of chopped cilantro, if you like.

The Greatest Crispy Smashed Potatoes

No matter how hard I may try, I just can't seem to shake my relentless craving for salty, crunchy potatoes. I love them in all the ways . . . frenched and fried, chipped, hash browned, tater totted, and so on. When it comes to making them myself, things get a little tricky, as frying foods isn't exactly simple or weeknight-friendly, and making homemade chips and/or tater tots requires a sort of patience and ability to not burn something that I don't always possess. But these crispy potatoes? They're like little problem-solvers, sweeping in to brighten your busy days and free you from having to fry, slice, or dice anything at all. The trick is using pre-roasted potatoes from your store (this saves us a ton of time and effort). Using your palm, just smash them down into your baking sheet and douse them in olive oil and a good amount of salt and pepper. Those mushy broken-seeming parts will transform into the brown, salty, crunchy bits that, let's be honest, are what we all came for in the first place.

SERVES 4

APPROXIMATE TIME: 50 MINUTES
   (ALMOST ENTIRELY HANDS-OFF)

30 to 35 ounces seasoned, roasted potatoes (see Note)

¼ cup olive oil

2 teaspoons Creole seasoning (optional)

Salt

Freshly ground black pepper

½ cup chopped fresh dill or parsley, for topping (optional)

Adjust the oven rack to the middle position, and preheat to 425 degrees F.

Arrange the potatoes on a baking sheet. Using your palm, smash the potatoes until they begin to split and break open, flattening them as much as you can and stopping just shy of breaking them totally apart.

Pour over the olive oil (¼ cup is usually the right amount, but you can use more if needed). Season with Creole seasoning (if using) and a little salt and lots of pepper. (Tip: taste a potato to see how salty it is before seasoning at all, as most pre-roasted potatoes are seasoned fairly well.) Give them all a good toss, and don't worry at all if they continue to break down and fall to pieces—this is actually a very good thing.

Roast for about 45 minutes, turning halfway through, until very browned and crispy. Serve with fresh chopped herbs on top if you like.

Note: All grocery stores sell pre-roasted potatoes in one form or another. I get mine in the refrigerated foods section, but in many cases, the deli/prepared foods and/or the frozen foods sections will carry them as well.

A Mashed Potato Revival

There may be no better example of just how quick and easy it can be to doctor up a store-bought item than these mashed potatoes. Firstly, store-bought mashers have come a long way since their instant dried flakes days. Yes, our stores now offer prepared mashed potatoes that, with just a little wave of our magic wand, can be elevated into something truly great. My family does this all the time, because the time-saving aspect of these revived potatoes is just so valuable. We can skip right ahead to the good part of things, where we conjure all the buttery, rich, homemade (tasting) decadence that we've all come to expect from our mashed potatoes. This is the fastest, most delicious way to get there, and like the little black dress, they really do go with everything.

SERVES 4 AS A SIDE

APPROXIMATE TIME: 25 MINUTES

5 tablespoons butter

1 tablespoon olive oil

5 whole sage leaves

1 teaspoon garlic powder

1 (32-ounce) container prepared mashed potatoes

½ cup sour cream or crème fraîche

Combine the butter and oil in a medium pot over medium heat. When the butter is melted, add the sage leaves and let them simmer and "frizzle" for 4 to 5 minutes, until they're lightly browned. Transfer them to a plate and leave that flavored butter right where it is.

Add the garlic powder to the sage-infused butter, and stir to sort of melt it in. Add the potatoes and the sour cream and stir to blend it all together. Allow the potatoes to heat all the way through over low heat for 8 to 10 minutes, uncovered (this will reduce some excess moisture, thickening the potatoes a bit).

Serve the potatoes hot, topped with some of the frizzled sage leaves, if you like.

Note: This recipe is like a great base camp, a starting point from which you can explore and take your potatoes to great new heights. The addition of some shredded or crumbled cheese is never not a nice idea. I love sharp cheddar, goat cheese, and/or blue cheese myself, depending on my mood. Also? A little bit of cream cheese, instead of the sour cream, is wonderful, as is the addition of some fresh minced garlic (instead of garlic powder), right after you've melted the butter.

Buttered Kimchi and Beet Oven-Fried Rice

SERVES 6 TO 8

APPROXIMATE TIME: 45 MINUTES

¼ cup soy sauce, plus more for serving

1 tablespoon rice vinegar

1 teaspoon garlic powder

⅓ cup store-bought honey-ginger salad dressing

¼ cup vegetable oil

1 (15-ounce) can julienned beets, chopped, liquid reserved

6 tablespoons butter, melted

30 to 32 ounces instant jasmine rice (3 packages)

1 cup frozen peas

1 cup frozen corn

1 cup shredded carrots

1 shallot, thinly sliced

1 cup store-bought kimchi, drained and chopped

Serving suggestions: chopped cilantro, chopped scallion greens and whites, toasted sesame seeds, Roasted Shrimp with Creamy Chili-Garlic Sauce (page 181)

The best crispy and fried rices are usually made with day-old rice. It's drier, past its prime, and therefore perfect fodder for doctoring up into something new. Just as banana bread is best with nearly black bananas and bread pudding is best with stale bread, some recipes are amazing grounds for second chances. That is, only if you happen to have those things lying around. I never (ever) have extra day-old rice just around—we eat it all, all of the time. So, for me to access that same premade quality when I want to whip up fried rice, I reach for the easy instant stuff. For applications like this, it's really pretty great. Plus? We're not actually frying it at all. If ever there was a perfect recipe to "sheet pan," it's fried rice. The rice and veggies are spread onto a highly buttered pan, maximizing the chances for crispiness, which is my favorite part. And the beets are honestly just beautiful here, adding their subtle, blushed hue and earth-rich voice to the chorus of vegetal sweetness from the peas, carrots, and corn. A sweetness that, incidentally, I happen to love when paired with the funky, umami-rich kimchi and the balancing richness of butter. Some matches are made in heaven. Others, it turns out, are made on humble baking sheets.

Preheat the oven to 475 degrees F.

In a small bowl or liquid measuring cup, combine the soy sauce, vinegar, garlic powder, salad dressing, vegetable oil, and the liquid from the can of beets. Set aside.

Coat a large baking sheet with the butter (it's a lot, on purpose).

In a large bowl, toss together the beets, rice, peas, corn, carrots, shallot, kimchi, and the reserved sauce.

Spread in an even layer on the buttered baking sheet, being sure to press it down. Bake for 18 to 20 minutes. Stir, scraping up any crispy browned bits, and place back in the oven to cook for 6 to 8 minutes more.

Top with cilantro and chopped scallion greens and whites, if you like. Serve with extra soy sauce on the side, for seasoning.

Note: This is really great served or topped with Roasted Shrimp with Creamy Chili-Garlic Sauce on page 181.

Cold Soba Noodles with Sprouts and Edamame

SERVES 4

APPROXIMATE TIME: 10 MINUTES

½ cup store-bought honey-ginger or sesame-ginger dressing

2 tablespoons Japanese or regular mayonnaise

1 tablespoon soy sauce

1 teaspoon garlic powder

8 ounces soba noodles

½ English cucumber, thinly sliced

1 or 2 watermelon radishes, thinly sliced (or 4 to 5 regular radishes)

2 cups shelled frozen edamame, thawed

2 cups watercress

8 ounces bean sprouts

It isn't random, the ingredients mixed and matched together from one recipe to the next here. Though to be honest, sometimes reading through recipes can sort of feel that way, right? Why, you may wonder, is she pairing these specific things together? Because it looks cool? Sounds cool? Did I spin the wheel-o'-ingredients and just go with whatever it told me to use? No, though that sounds like it could be somewhat fun. I've had readers ask me questions about this before, about ingredient selection and how it all comes to fruition. I rarely ever work in a straight line, but there is a greater intention underlying the recipes I share. There is rhyme and there is reason, always. For this extremely simple noodle bowl, the chewy Japanese-style buckwheat (soba) noodles get a textural boost from some cold, snappy bean sprouts, sliced cucumber, and edamame. A slightly doctored store-bought ginger dressing ties it all together, perfectly accenting each bite of this refreshing, noodle salad.

Start by making the dressing. In a bowl, stir together the honey-ginger dressing, mayonnaise, soy sauce, and garlic powder.

Prepare the noodles according to the package directions. Drain, and toss them with as much of the dressing as you like. Divide between four serving bowls. Top with cucumber slices, radish slices, edamame, watercress, and bean sprouts. Serve with extra dressing on the side.

Pan-Fried Cornbread with Burst Harissa Tomatoes and Butter Beans

I suppose you could say that this one was inspired by avocado toast because, well, it was. Call it an unpopular opinion, but I've truly never understood the immense popularity of avo toast. While I like it just fine, it's never knocked either one of my socks off. To each their own, though. But this toast? She speaks to my soul. A humble store-bought loaf of cornbread is sliced and pan-fried in lots of fruity olive oil, and then topped with a deeply flavorful sauce made from burst tomatoes, spicy harissa (see Note), and almost too much garlic. Giant, creamy beans escort this dish out of "almost enough" territory into a place of total satisfaction.

SERVES 4

APPROXIMATE TIME: 25 MINUTES

3 to 4 tablespoons olive oil, plus more as needed

1 loaf cornbread, cut into ¼- or ⅓-inch planks

1 pint cherry tomatoes, halved

Salt

Freshly ground black pepper

2 to 3 tablespoons harissa paste or sauce (see Note)

3 large garlic cloves, minced

1 (15-ounce) can butter beans, drained and rinsed (any white bean will work)

Serving suggestions: ½ to ¾ cup fresh chopped green herbs, such as parsley, chives, and/or thyme

Heat a couple tablespoons of olive oil in a large skillet over medium heat. Working in batches, toast the cornbread slices for about 2 minutes per side, until very golden brown on each side. You can add more oil in between batches and as needed. Transfer the toasted cornbread to serving plates or a tray and hold in a warm oven (170 degrees F) while you prepare the sauce.

Add 2 more tablespoons of oil to the pan, along with the tomatoes. Season with salt and pepper and cook for 6 to 7 minutes, until they've burst and have released their juices.

Add the harissa, garlic, and beans, stir, and cook for another 5 minutes. Serve the sauce spooned over the toasted cornbread, and top with green herbs if you like.

Note: Harissa is a North African pepper-based sauce, paste, or sometimes dried-spice blend. Beautifully warm and quite spicy, it's widely available in the international aisles of most American supermarkets. But if you can't find it, it can be omitted. Asian-style chili garlic sauce makes a good substitution. If you want a great way to use the rest of your harissa, add a tablespoon or two to the poaching liquid in Buttery Poached Fish with Fennel and Tomatoes (page 180) or in place of the red curry paste in Red Curry Mac and Cheese (page 123), which just happens to be the next recipe.

Red Curry Mac and Cheese

SERVES 4 TO 6

APPROXIMATE TIME: < 30 MINUTES

1 pound short-cut pasta (I use cavatappi, but just use what you like)

Salt

3 tablespoons ghee, butter, or coconut oil

2-inch piece fresh ginger, peeled and minced or grated

3 large garlic cloves, minced or grated

¼ cup plus 1 tablespoon all-purpose flour

4 ounces prepared Thai-style red curry paste

Freshly ground black pepper

1 (13.5-ounce) can coconut milk

1 cup milk

8 ounces shredded white cheddar cheese

8 ounces shredded mozzarella (pre-shredded is okay here)

8 ounces shredded fontina (optional)

Serving suggestions: chopped cilantro, scallions, Thai-basil, chopped peanuts

I'm never not looking for ways to sneak Thai-style red curry paste into my cooking. The ratio of flavor payoff to effort is so very appealing—it just makes everything it touches taste so much better, without having to do any work at all. It's a true pantry staple, a homemade-ish mainstay to be sure. And while I enjoy using it in many a Thai-style recipe, I've actually been stirring this flavorful, vermilion-hued paste into my quick-fix stovetop mac and cheese and let me just say . . . wow. It's hard to imagine mac and cheese any other way now to be honest. What has, to me, classically been a dish that is just okay (I know, hot take there), is now something I crave on the regular.

Cook the pasta to al dente according to package directions in salty water (like the sea). Drain and set aside.

Meanwhile, in a large skillet over medium heat, heat the ghee, along with the ginger and garlic. Cook, stirring, for about 1 minute. Sprinkle the flour over top and cook, stirring, for another minute. Add the curry paste and stir to blend it in. Season with salt and pepper to taste.

Whisk in the coconut milk and allow things to come up to a gentle bubble, stirring well to combine. Whisk in the cup of milk. Turn off the heat and stir in all of the cheeses including the fontina (if using) until creamy and smooth. Taste the sauce and season to your liking. Add the pasta into the skillet and stir to coat.

Serve the mac and cheese with some chopped cilantro, scallions, and/or Thai basil on top and, if you like, some chopped peanuts. Enjoy right away.

Note: To reheat, just add a little more milk to the pan to loosen the sauce and warm over low heat until smooth.

Pasta Rags with Peas, Burrata, and Crisped Prosciutto

"Pasta Rags" has such a charming ring to it, a ring that may only be outshone by how very simple these are to whip up. This is just a way to change up how we serve some basic lasagna noodles, ripping and cutting them into shaggy "rags" rather than laboriously layering them up in a pan with multiple sauces and other various flotsam (no offense, lasagna—I do love you). Not only does this recipe make interesting use of those noodles, it also has a very simple sauce built from little more than some store-bought chive and onion cream cheese that has been thinned out with a little starchy, salty pasta water. The burrata is optional, as it is a little splurgy I'll admit, but its creaminess melds with that simple sauce, blurring the lines between things a bit. Sweet peas fight with salty prosciutto for top billing in this fork-and-knife pasta dish, but are really better together here, stealing the show as happy costars in this true rags-to-riches tale.

SERVES 4

APPROXIMATE TIME: < 30 MINUTES

1 pound lasagna noodles

2 tablespoons olive oil, divided, plus more as needed

6 slices prosciutto

1 teaspoon vegetable or chicken stock concentrate (I like Better than Bouillon)

1 bunch scallions, chopped, white and green parts separated

1 cup frozen green peas

4 ounces chive and onion cream cheese

Salt

Freshly ground black pepper

1 (8-ounce) ball burrata cheese

Zest of 2 lemons

Cook the lasagna noodles in salted water according to package instructions. Reserve 1 cup of the starchy cooking water before draining. Transfer the noodles to a flat surface and either cut or tear them into smaller pieces of different sizes and shapes (you can also do this right in the pot, honestly). "Rags" implies intentional imperfection, so rip, shred, and cut as you please here. You can drizzle the noodles with a little olive oil to keep them from sticking if you like.

Add 1 tablespoon of olive oil to a large skillet over medium heat. Add the prosciutto, in batches as needed, and cook for 2 to 3 minutes per side, until they begin to seize up and brown. Transfer the prosciutto to a plate or tray and don't wipe out the pan.

Add the remaining 1 tablespoon of oil to the pan, along with the stock concentrate, scallion whites, and the peas (no need to thaw). Cook, stirring, for about 1 minute. Add the cream cheese and about ½ cup of the starchy pasta water. Cook, stirring, just until the cream cheese has melted into a smooth sauce. Taste and season with salt and pepper.

Add the pasta to the pan with the sauce and toss to coat as best you can. Divide the pasta and creamy peas among individual plates or you can pile it all onto a big platter. Top with pieces of the crispy prosciutto and some big torn pieces of creamy burrata. Finish with a drizzle of olive oil, the lemon zest, and the scallion greens.

Poultry

Spatchcocked Chicken Marbella

This updated version of the popular 1980s recipe is the perfect opportunity to ask your butcher to spatchcock a chicken for you. It only takes six ingredients and still turns out so fantastically delicious—my favorite roasted chicken ever. Furthermore, it also gets you to use prunes, which are deserving of far more attention than they get in most weeknight kitchens. Were you to swap them out for dates, you'd end up with a very North African–style tagine type of dish. If you chose, instead, to use golden raisins, you'd get something resembling a Sicilian caponata. But the women who wrote the beloved *Silver Palate Cookbook* in 1979 opted to use prunes, and so shall we.

SERVES 4

APPROXIMATE TIME: 45 TO 50
  MINUTES

3 tablespoons olive oil, divided,
  plus more as needed

1 whole chicken, spatchcocked
  (see Note)

Salt

Freshly ground black pepper

8 ounces prunes, divided

7 to 8 ounces pitted green
  olives, drained, divided

4 garlic cloves, smashed,
  divided

⅓ cup plus 1 tablespoon red
  wine vinegar

½ cup white wine

Serving suggestions: sliced
  shallots (optional), a handful
  of coarsely chopped green
  herbs such as fresh basil,
  parsley, dill, and/or chives

Adjust the oven rack to the middle position, and preheat to 400 degrees F.

Heat 2 tablespoons olive oil in a large, deep-sided, ovenproof pan set over medium-high to high heat. Season the chicken generously with salt and pepper. Brown the chicken, skin-side down, for 6 to 8 minutes. Don't touch or move it! That will deter the best browning. Transfer the chicken to a platter or baking sheet. Don't wipe out the pan.

Meanwhile, while the chicken is browning, combine 4 of the prunes, ½ cup of the olives, 1 garlic clove, 1 tablespoon olive oil, and 1 tablespoon of the vinegar in a food processor or blender. Process or blend until a smooth creamy spread/paste forms. Set aside.

Reduce the heat on the stove to medium. Add the wine, ⅓ cup of vinegar, 3 smashed garlic cloves, and the remaining prunes and olives to the pan and stir well. Stir in 1 tablespoon of the reserved prune/olive paste. Scrape up all of the browned bits on the bottom of the pan and allow the sauce to bubble and reduce for 3 or 4 minutes.

Transfer the chicken to the pan, skin-side up, and slather the remaining prune/olive paste all over the top. Roast for 15 minutes.

Reduce the oven temperature to 350 degrees F, and roast for 18 to 20 minutes more, or until the chicken is done in the center (165 degrees F).

Serve the chicken with the pan sauce, garnished with sliced shallots if you like, and a handful of the green herbs of your choice.

Note: This bears repeating, partly because it's such a good thing to know, and also because I know everyone doesn't read every word in a cookbook. You may have breezed right over the info on page 17 which is, of course, just fine. So, I'm saying it again: the easiest way to spatchcock a chicken (i.e. remove its backbone), is to simply ask the folks at the butcher counter to do it for you. Or, even better, find one that has already been done, as they're fairly widely available.

Firecracker Fried-Chicken Noodle Soup

A homemade-ish spin on one of the most popular recipes I have ever shared, this is chicken noodle soup with its party pants on. By taking the chicken out of the soup and piling it on top in a heap of crispy, spicy fried goodness, we change the very notion of what chicken noodle soup has to be. Who says you can't rearrange a classic? We'll take some help from the grocery store's deli section and use premade popcorn chicken, chicken tenders, or nuggets and coat them in an addictively sweet and spicy sauce that brings the whole pot of soup to life.

SERVES 4

APPROXIMATE TIME: 25 MINUTES

⅔ cup Frank's hot sauce, or something comparable

¼ cup honey

¼ cup soy sauce

1½ to 2 pounds premade popcorn chicken from your grocer's deli/prepared foods section

1 to 2 tablespoons olive oil

2 large carrots, sliced

3 celery stalks, finely diced

1½ cups diced onion

1½ tablespoons poultry seasoning

1½ teaspoons garlic powder

Salt

Freshly ground black pepper

32-ounces chicken stock

¼ cup garlic-and-herb cheese spread, give or take (such as Boursin or Alouette)

1 (12-ounce) package homestyle or regular egg noodles

Serving suggestion: crumbled blue cheese

Adjust the oven rack to the middle position, and preheat to 425 degrees F.

Combine the hot sauce, honey, and soy sauce in a small skillet over medium heat. Bring to a simmer and stir until well mixed. Simmer gently for a few minutes to thicken and reduce. You can add more of any ingredient to suit your taste (and if you want *more sauce*).

Place the chicken on a large baking sheet and pour the firecracker sauce all over the top. Toss the chicken until thoroughly coated in the sauce. Bake for just 4 to 5 minutes to crisp up. Keep warm until ready to serve.

To make the soup, heat about 1 tablespoon of oil to a large, deep skillet set over medium-high heat. Add the carrots, celery, onion, poultry seasoning, and garlic powder. Season lightly with salt and pepper. Reduce the heat to medium and cook for about 5 minutes, until the veggies are tender.

Add the stock and the cheese spread and stir to combine. Add the noodles and simmer until they are just cooked through. They will release their starches and really thicken the soup. If you like a thinner soup, you can add more stock, water, or milk until the consistency is to your liking.

Serve right away (because the noodles will drink the liquid), spooned into bowls and topped with the crispy firecracker chicken. (I like to serve it with a little crumbled blue cheese.)

Pretzel Chicken with Creamy Beer Cheese

Am I giving you a recipe for chicken tenders? Yes, I'm doing that. But honestly, I don't think we ever grow out of our childhood affections for crunchy, salty, golden-brown chicken, made all the better for whatever creamy sauce gets to come along for the ride. I've been making this chicken for the longest time, and it's great as a starter or an app (perfect for watching all of the sports), but it's also really good piled on top of a salad. We're not frying anything here, as I've found these are just as good when you bake them, not to mention much easier. The creamy, three-ingredient beer cheese is an ode to my Kentucky roots. The dip is highly revered in that state, as it should be. It's addictively delicious, and the perfect accompaniment for anything pretzel-adjacent, namely this chicken.

SERVES 6

APPROXIMATE TIME: 35 MINUTES

1 (16-ounce) bag seasoned pretzels (such as Dot's)

24 to 28 ounces boneless, skinless chicken breast tenderloins

Salt

Freshly ground black pepper

8 ounces sour cream

8 ounces sharp cheddar cheese

4 ounces light-bodied beer (you may have to drink the rest)

½ teaspoon garlic powder

Adjust the oven rack to the middle position, and preheat to 400 degrees F.

Crush the pretzels until they're (mostly) finely ground in whatever manner you like. I opt to put them in my food processor and blitz them until very finely ground. But you could also just crush them right in the bag they came in if you like. Whatever works for you here.

Season the chicken with salt and pepper. Put the sour cream in a shallow bowl or plate and thin with about 2 tablespoons of water. Dip each tender in the sour cream, shaking off any excess, and then dredge through the pretzel crumbs, coating fully. You can do this right in the food processor, but be sure to remove the blade first. Clean out the food processor when you're finished.

Arrange the chicken on a large baking sheet and bake for about 20 minutes, until cooked through and deeply golden brown (an internal temperature of 165 degrees F, if you're measuring).

Meanwhile, put the cheese into the food processor and process for about a minute until broken up and mostly smooth. Add the beer and continue processing until very smooth and creamy. Season with salt and the garlic powder, and transfer to a bowl. This will firm up as it sits. Serve alongside the warm chicken tenders, for dipping.

Note: Kentucky-style beer cheese is not cooked, so there is some alcohol content going on there, though it's minimal. If you don't care for the taste of beer or want an alcohol-free cheese dip instead, you can simply swap in vegetable stock, chicken stock, or even water. Or, just use ranch dressing for dipping.

Chicken with 40 Cloves of Garlic

I love it when a recipe is also a great conversation starter. This one always manages to garner plenty of intrigued commentary from diners when you set it down on the table. Forty cloves is not a small number—it's not subtle is it? No, it is not. And therein lies the greatness of this dish (which I did not invent). I've always said that anytime I list a number of garlic cloves in a recipe, that it should be treated as the minimum amount—as in, use *at least* two cloves, etc. Here though, I'd say forty is about right. This is an easy yet elegant chicken recipe that highlights the natural flavor-enhancing powers of garlic, which softens, sweetens, and mellows as it cooks in the wine-laced broth, making it eat more like butter in the end. This is the very best time to go ahead and reach for those packs of pre-peeled garlic cloves. While they often go bad before I can use all of the cloves, majorly garlic-heavy recipes like this are absolutely the place to use those very time-saving bags of garlic.

SERVES 4

APPROXIMATE TIME: 45 MINUTES

2 tablespoon olive oil

4 bone-in skin-on chicken thighs

6 to 8 chicken drumsticks

Salt

Freshly ground black pepper

2 tablespoons butter

1 small onion, diced

2 celery stalks, diced

2 bay leaves

40 whole garlic cloves (I recommend purchasing a bag of pre-peeled garlic)

1 cup dry white wine

1 cup chicken stock

1 tablespoon cornstarch or flour

Serving suggestions: Simple Arugula Salad (page 86), or watercress, and crusty bread for sopping

Adjust the oven rack to the middle position, and preheat to 350 degrees F.

Heat the oil in a large Dutch oven over medium-high heat. Season the chicken pieces very well with salt and pepper. When the oil is shimmering hot, brown the chicken on both sides for 3 to 4 minutes per side, until the skin is nice and crispy. Transfer the browned chicken to a tray or plate.

Reduce the heat to medium and add the butter to the pot. Add the onion, celery, bay leaves, and garlic and cook, stirring, for 4 to 5 minutes, until the veggies are tender. Add the wine and stock and stir to get up any browned bits. In a small bowl, stir together the cornstarch with some of the hot cooking liquid from the pot, creating a smooth paste with no lumps. Pour this mixture (called a slurry) back into the pot and stir, making sure no lumps form (this will lightly thicken the sauce).

Nestle the chicken down into the pot, ensuring that each piece is about halfway submerged.

Put the lid on the pot and place in the oven. Bake for 25 to 30 minutes, or until the chicken is tender. Remove the lid, turn on the broiler to high, and broil for 3 to 4 minutes, until the chicken skin is visibly browned and crispy (keep an eye on it to avoid burning!).

To serve, I like to transfer the chicken to a big platter and spoon the sauce all around the pieces, really putting all of that garlic on display. Top with Simple Arugula Salad or some peppery watercress.

Note: Need another way to use up the rest of the bag of garlic? Try the Italian Wedding Soup with Roasted Garlic Broth (page 74).

French Onion Chicken and Potatoes Skillet

Talk about a pan of food that I could basically live in. This six-ingredient concoction is kind of like if Irish nachos were to wed French onion soup in a ceremony presided over by . . . a chicken. Yes, that's exactly it. I love a good French onion–flavored anything, really, from mac and cheese to burgers and patty melts, giving anything the French onion treatment is almost always a good idea. Here, we'll shingle a whole mess of waffle fries (the homemade-ish part) over the saucy, oniony chicken and then shower it all with salty, nutty Gruyère or Swiss cheese and bake until gooey and crispy all at once.

SERVES 4

APPROXIMATE TIME: 35 MINUTES

Olive oil for cooking

6 boneless, skinless chicken thighs

Salt

Freshly ground black pepper

5 small sweet onions, thinly sliced

1½ tablespoons coarse-grain Dijon mustard

2 to 3 cups beef stock

1 (20-ounce) package frozen waffle fries, baked 5 minutes less than directed on the package

2 cups shredded Gruyère cheese (Swiss can be subbed)

Adjust the oven rack to the middle position, and preheat to 425 degrees F.

Heat a couple tablespoons of olive oil in a large ovenproof skillet set over medium-high heat. When it's hot, add the chicken thighs, season generously with salt and pepper, and brown well on both sides, a few minutes per side. Transfer to a plate or tray and don't clean out the pan.

Reduce the heat to medium, add the sliced onions, season lightly with salt and pepper, and cook for 10 to 12 minutes, stirring frequently, until tender and soft. Add the mustard and 2 cups of the stock and stir to combine. Add more stock if needed to fully submerge the onions.

Slide the chicken back into the pan, along with all of the juices (liquid gold!). Scatter the prebaked waffle fries all over top in a big layer (you may not use all of them, up to you). Cover with the shredded cheese and bake for 12 to 15 minutes, until golden and bubbling. I like to broil for the last couple of minutes to get things nice and crispy.

Note: the number of onions you use here doesn't need to be exact. My onions were very small, so I used six. But two really big, softball-size ones would probably work fine. You just want a thick layer of sliced onions to cover the whole pan. They will cook down a ton, so just keep that in mind.

Chicken and Chorizo Enchilada Bake

SERVES 4

APPROXIMATE TIME: 35 MINUTES

1 tablespoon cooking oil, plus more for brushing

1 small yellow onion, sliced

1 (9-ounce) package Mexican-style raw bulk chorizo, not dried links (see Note on page 187)

1 teaspoon ground cumin

1 teaspoon chili powder

2 teaspoons smoked paprika

4 garlic cloves, minced or grated

1 rotisserie chicken, meat shredded or chopped

1 (28-ounce) can low-sodium red enchilada sauce

Salt

Freshly ground black pepper

10 to 12 small corn tortillas, cut into quarters

3 cups shredded Mexican Cheese blend

Crumbled cotija or feta cheese (optional)

Serving suggestions: sliced avocados, sour cream, pickled jalapeños, cilantro

This ultrasimple enchilada skillet recipe reminds me of a savory Tex-Mex version of a dump cake, as the ingredients are more or less just dumped in the skillet, cooked until hot and bubbly, et voilà—dinner is served. Put another way, this is also very much a smashup of enchiladas and chilaquiles, two of my all-time favorite Mexican dishes. Though in our homemade-ish spin, we'll elevate a jar of red enchilada sauce for a truly speedy-simple version. When you've got spicy chorizo and loads of fresh garlic at play, you'd really have to make a huge mistake for it to even come close to being bad. In the spirit of my beloved Ina Garten, this is truly a "how bad can it be?" recipe of the highest order.

Adjust the oven rack to the middle position, and preheat to 375 degrees F.

Heat the oil in a large ovenproof skillet set over medium heat. When it's hot, add the onion and chorizo and cook, stirring occasionally and breaking up the chorizo, for 5 to 6 minutes, until the onion is tender.

Add the cumin, chili powder, smoked paprika, and garlic and cook, stirring, for about 30 seconds. Stir in the chicken and the enchilada sauce. Taste and if you think it needs it, season lightly with salt and pepper (chorizo is salty so you may not).

Add about half of the tortilla pieces to the skillet and stir to mix them in. Shingle the rest on top and brush/rub lightly with oil (the exact number of tortillas you use can vary—just whatever you like). Top with a few handfuls of the Mexican cheese (I never measure this—a few cups is good), and some feta or cotija, if you like.

Bake, uncovered, for 12 to 16 minutes, until bubbly and golden brown. Top with whatever you like and enjoy warm.

Puffy Chicken Pot Pie

So, my mom was visiting when I first tested this recipe, and she immediately declared it to be the best puffy chicken pot pie she'd ever had. Accounting for her big-time mom bias and the fact that I don't believe she's ever actually had a puffy chicken pot pie, take that as you will. I use shredded rotisserie chicken, smoked chicken sausage, frozen vegetables, and crème fraîche as my quick-fix tricks here. The addition of sautéed onion, garlic, and fresh thyme brings necessary freshness to the dish, helping us to totally fool all who try it.

SERVES 4

APPROXIMATE TIME: 30 MINUTES

2 tablespoons olive oil

1 small onion, chopped

4 links smoked chicken sausage, cut into bite-size pieces

3 garlic cloves, minced

1 (10- to 12-ounce) bag frozen peas and carrots

1 rotisserie chicken, shredded (both light and dark meat)

4 to 6 ounces crème fraîche or cream cheese

1 to 1½ cups chicken stock

1 to 2 teaspoons fresh thyme leaves, lightly chopped or not

Salt

Freshly ground black pepper

1 teaspoon poultry seasoning or Old Bay seasoning

1 egg (optional)

1 sheet of puff pastry (from a 17-ounce package), thawed

Adjust the oven rack to the middle position, and preheat to 400 degrees F.

Heat the oil in a large ovenproof skillet over medium heat. When it's hot, add the onion and sausage, and sauté for about 5 minutes. Add the garlic and peas and carrots and cook, stirring occasionally, until thawed.

Add the shredded chicken, crème fraîche, stock, and thyme. Stir to combine and season with salt and pepper, as well as the poultry seasoning. If you like, you can transfer the filling to a pie plate or, just leave it right in the ovenproof skillet.

For an extra golden-brown crust, in a small bowl, beat together the egg and 1 tablespoon of water. Place a sheet of puff pastry on a baking sheet and brush to coat with a layer of this egg wash (see Note 2). Place the pie plate or skillet in the oven, along with the baking sheet. Bake for 15 to 20 minutes, until the pastry is brilliantly puffy and the filling is bubbly and hot.

Place the pastry on top of the filling before serving.

Note 1: Baking the pastry separately results in a very crispy, puffy crust. You could bake it right on top of the filling, but it won't rise near as much, and the shattering crunch effect will be lost. It will still taste great, though.

Note 2: You can create any shape or style of crust you'd like here. You can slice the pastry into strips and lattice them together. Or, keep them in long strips, or just use as a large whole sheet of pastry, no cutting required.

Marry Me Chicken

SERVES 4

APPROXIMATE TIME: 30 TO 35
  MINUTES

**6 boneless, skinless chicken
thighs or 2 breasts, halved
crosswise**

Salt

Freshly ground black pepper

2 tablespoons cooking oil

1 cup diced onion

2 tablespoons butter

2 tablespoons all-purpose flour

**3 garlic cloves, minced or
grated**

**⅔ cup dry white wine (optional,
but highly recommended)**

**2 teaspoons chicken stock
concentrate (I like Better
Than Bouillon)**

**⅓ cup sun-dried tomato spread,
sun-dried tomato pesto, or
drained sun-dried tomatoes
(see Note)**

**½ cup half-and-half or heavy
cream**

**1 cup shredded or torn fontina
cheese**

**Fresh basil or watercress, for
topping**

**Serving suggestions: This is
good with and on everything,
so just grab your carb of
choice (rice, orzo, pasta of
any shape, quinoa, etc.) and
enjoy.**

Not to be confused with marry me, chicken. My version of Marry Me Chicken is Italian through and through, a nod to my own roots and favorite ingredients: sun-dried tomatoes, garlic, white wine, olive oil, and fontina cheese. It's just to-die-for good, and it checks all of the major homemade-ish boxes for ease, efficiency, and affordability. Supposedly named for its utter deliciousness and for how well the ingredients "marry together," Marry Me Chicken is a cheeky little dish, one that really does shine. I've always been in a love affair with sun-dried tomatoes. They're so very flavorful, in this piquant, sweet-tangy way that really is only theirs to claim. I hoard them apocalyptically, just stacking the jars in tidy glass towers in the recesses of my pantry. When coupled with fontina cheese and a splash of white wine, you've got yourself a nice union indeed.

Season the chicken all over with salt and pepper. Heat oil in a large skillet over medium-high heat. Brown the chicken for 3 to 4 minutes per side, until golden. Transfer to a plate (it will finish cooking later).

Reduce the heat to medium and don't wipe out the skillet. Add the onion and sauté for a few minutes to tenderize in the drippings. Add the butter and the flour, along with the garlic. Cook, stirring, for about 1 minute. Add the wine and cook for another minute or so. Add the stock concentrate, the sun-dried tomato spread, 1½ cups of water, the cream, and the cheese and stir to thoroughly combine, until the cheese melts. It shouldn't need much more salt, but taste and season as you like.

Slide the chicken back into the pan, along with all the juices. Simmer for a minute or so, or until it's cooked through. (This makes a lot of sauce, which is not an accident.)

Top with a shower of watercress or fresh basil and serve the saucy chicken over anything you like (rice or pasta are my go-tos, depending on what I need to use up).

Note: Sun-dried tomatoes are often sold in a few forms, ranging from straight-up and packed in oil to pestos and spreads. Any one you choose will work beautifully here. If you are unable to find the sun-dried tomato spread or a sun-dried tomato pesto (which work best since they're already in spread/paste form), no worries! You can substitute a drained 7-ounce jar of sun-dried tomatoes. Just finely chop or even pro-cess or blend them until they're more of a smooth, paste-like consistency, adding water as needed to achieve this. Use in the recipe as instructed.

Honeymoon Chicken

The **only** recipe that can logically follow in the footsteps of Marry Me Chicken is this utterly delicious Honeymoon Chicken. They're similar in some ways—both being saucy chicken skillets that only require one pan to pull off. But they diverge from one another in some key ways, too, namely via the use of bone-in versus boneless chicken. Here, bone-in meat adds richness and juiciness to everything, bolstering the sauce and flavoring the potatoes more deeply. And the sauce is something else entirely. Tangy buttermilk, earthy-sweet beets, and some store-bought red pepper hummus combine into a sauce made even better by the addition of spicy Calabrian chiles. Why do we call it Honeymoon Chicken? Because it's spicy, everything gets along so very well together, and if you close your eyes when you enjoy your first bite, you might feel a little like you're vacationing in a gorgeous, sun-drenched Mediterranean villa, complete with resplendent grounds, faint notes of live music floating through the air, and perhaps a few friendly cats wandering around. Or maybe that's just me.

SERVES 4

APPROXIMATE TIME: 45 MINUTES

24 ounces gold potatoes, halved if they're "baby" or sliced into 6 wedges if larger

6 bone-in, skin-on chicken thighs (about 2½ pounds)

Salt

Freshly ground black pepper

1 tablespoon Italian or Mediterranean seasoning blend

3 tablespoons olive oil, plus more as needed

1 sweet onion, sliced

1 (15-ounce) can sliced beets, drained

1 tablespoon chopped Calabrian chiles (or 1 tablespoon sambal oelek)

10-ounces roasted red pepper hummus

2 cups full-fat buttermilk

Simple Arugula Salad (page 86), for topping

Adjust an oven rack to the middle position, and preheat to 400 degrees F.

Put the cut potatoes in a pot with water to cover and bring to a boil over high heat. Parboil for 10 minutes. Drain and set aside.

Meanwhile, season the chicken all over with salt, pepper, and the Italian or Mediterranean seasoning. Heat the oil in a large skillet set over medium-high heat.

When the oil is hot, brown the chicken on both sides for about 4 minutes per side, until golden (it will finish cooking in the oven). Transfer the chicken to a plate.

Reduce the heat to medium and don't worry about wiping out the pan. Add the onion and parboiled potatoes, season with salt and pepper, and cook in the rendered chicken fat for 6 to 8 minutes, stirring occasionally, until the onion is tender and the potatoes pick up a little color. You can add more olive oil, if necessary, to keep things from sticking.

Meanwhile, combine the beets, chiles, hummus, and buttermilk in a blender and blend until totally smooth. Season the spicy, rosy-hued sauce with salt and pepper to taste.

Place the chicken back in the pan, skin-side up, with the onions and potatoes. Pour the sauce all around the pan until it reaches about ¾ of the way to the top of the chicken, ensuring the skin stays dry. Roast for about 30 minutes, until the chicken is cooked through and the skin is golden brown and crispy (technically, it should register

an internal temperature of 165 degrees F on an instant-read thermometer).

Transfer the cooked chicken onto plates. Stir the potatoes and onions in the pan, coating them in the sauce. Serve the creamy potatoes alongside the chicken and top with Simple Arugula Salad (this brings the whole plate together).

Note: Calabrian chiles are a fiery, fruity pepper grown in Italy's southern region of Calabria. They're hugely flavorful, and my favorite way to add spice to so many dishes. Widely available in grocery stores' Italian sections, sometimes you'll find these chiles sold whole, jarred in oil or a marinade of sorts. Or, you may find them already chopped, saving you that step. A little goes a long way, and I find a tablespoon to be just right in this spicy sauce. You'll have leftovers, and they can be treated as you would a hot sauce or chili sauce.

Baked Turkey Smash Burgers

Get ready to never look at a burger the same way again. I am obsessed with cheeseburgers and often order them when I'm dining out. In fact, my most recent New Year's resolution was to sample all of the lauded cheeseburgers in my town. Cooking them at home, though? That tends to be a greasy, smelly enough affair to prevent me from ever wanting to mess with it. Until now. Enter my baked turkey burgers. I know, it really sounds odd but you're just going to have to trust me here. The burgers will cook in their own juices, all in one batch, keeping them juicy and your stovetop and kitchen much fresher. This is such a win.

MAKES 6 BURGERS
APPROXIMATE TIME: 30 MINUTES

1 tablespoon olive oil, plus more for brushing

2 pounds ground turkey (better to have more than not enough here)

2 teaspoons salt

Freshly ground black pepper

1 teaspoon garlic powder

6 potato buns

Topping suggestions: I keep it classic with American cheese, sliced red onion, sliced tomatoes, mayo, pickles, and crunchy lettuce.

Adjust the oven rack to the middle position, and preheat to 400 degrees F. Brush two large baking sheets with a layer of olive oil.

In a large bowl, combine the turkey, salt, lots of pepper, garlic powder, and the olive oil.

Hollow out the thick, doughy insides of your burger buns a little bit, and chop the pieces into fresh breadcrumbs. This doesn't have to be exact, but when you've got about ½ cup's worth, add those to the turkey mixture. Gently mix until everything is evenly combined (just don't overwork as this makes burgers dense).

Divide the mixture into 6 equal-size portions/balls and place them on the baking sheets. Smash each of the balls with your palm until they're about ⅓ inch thick and roughly 4 to 4½ inches across. Perfection need not apply here. Season them with a little more salt and pepper (2 pounds of turkey needs seasoning).

Bake the burgers for 11 to 12 minutes, until the meat is just cooked through and browned. When only 1 minute of cook time remains, carefully place a cheese slice on each patty. We're going for the opposite of dry hockey pucks here. If you're unsure whether your burgers are done or not, you can cut into one to see if the inside is no longer pink.

Serve the burgers right away on the buns with your preferred toppings and sauces. (*Note: I opted for a double cheeseburger in the photo, but these work great as singles or doubles.*)

Rachel Goes to Mumbai

(or, Curry Buttered Turkey Rachel Sandwiches with Green Chutney Slaw)

This one goes out to my cousin, Rachel, who loves sandwiches the very most—especially those which contain no traces of a tomato. As such, the classic Rachel sandwich appears to have been serendipitously named, as this saucy, gooey, warm dream of a sandwich seems like the perfect fit for her. In my version, we're going to take classic Rachel (turkey + Swiss + coleslaw) on a trip to India by toasting everything up in some curry butter. We'll also infuse store-bought coleslaw with loads of cilantro and mint, a nod to a classic Indian green chutney, which ranks among my favorite condiments in the world. When paired with that curry butter, the flavors truly do transport an otherwise simple and unassuming turkey sandwich into something that is otherworldly delicious.

MAKES 4 SANDWICHES

APPROXIMATE TIME: 30 MINUTES

8 tablespoons unsalted butter,
at room temperature

1 teaspoon curry powder

Salt

½ ounce fresh mint leaves

1 bunch fresh cilantro, both
leaves and stems

3 tablespoons olive oil

1 cup prepared shredded
coleslaw

1 pound sliced turkey

12 slices Swiss cheese

8 slices sourdough bread

Combine the butter and curry powder in a bowl and season with salt.

Combine the mint, cilantro, and olive oil in a blender or food processor and process until it's a homogeneous paste-like mixture. Add this to the coleslaw, using as much or as little as you like, stirring to blend.

To make one sandwich (you can also do several at a time, if you prefer): Set a large nonstick skillet over medium heat. Add a couple teaspoons of the curry butter and top with 3 or 4 slices of turkey and 3 slices of Swiss. Let the turkey brown on the bottom and the cheese melt a bit, browning and crisping up around the edges, 2 to 3 minutes. (You can put a lid on to expedite this, but I don't like to wash that extra dish, personally).

Meanwhile, evenly spread some of the chutney slaw across a slice of the bread.

Transfer the cheesy turkey pile to the bread, on top of the slaw. Put another piece of bread on top, and slather with the curry butter. Cook the sandwich, buttered-side down, for 1 to 1½ minutes until golden and crisp, lowering the heat a little if needed. Butter the other side before flipping to cook that as well.

Repeat with the rest of the sandwiches.

Slice and serve warm.

Cabbage Patch Chicken

This was the only logical name for this recipe, right? Resting on a bed of what are essentially tiny cabbages, these chicken thighs don't know how good they've got it. I've been making versions of this recipe for a while now, and find that people really kind of go wild for it. Must be the honey mustard—its sweetness balances the inherent funk of those Brussels sprouts like they were meant to be together. Or, actually, maybe it's the pecan crumble. The crunch and toasty, ever-so-faint cinnamon note it adds just really lands the plane for us here. And by plane I mean chicken. It lands the chicken.

SERVES 4

APPROXIMATE TIME: < 45 MINUTES

⅔ cup chopped pecans

½ cup old-fashioned oats

½ teaspoon ground cinnamon

½ teaspoon salt, plus more as needed

½ cup plus 2 tablespoons all-purpose flour, divided

5 tablespoons olive oil, divided

6 boneless, skinless chicken thighs

Freshly ground black pepper

3 cups (give or take) Brussels sprouts, halved

1 cup store-bought honey-mustard salad dressing

2 teaspoons chicken stock concentrate (I like Better Than Bouillon)

Preheat the oven to 350 degrees F.

On a large baking sheet, combine the pecans, oats, cinnamon, salt, 2 tablespoons of flour, and 2 tablespoons of olive oil. Toss with your hands to evenly coat everything and bake, stirring halfway through, for 10 to 12 minutes, or until the pecans are deep golden brown. Remove from the oven and set aside.

Meanwhile, in a large skillet over medium-high heat, heat 2 tablespoons of oil. Season the chicken thighs with salt and pepper and dredge them in the remaining ½ cup of flour, giving them a thin coating. Cook the chicken for 3 to 4 minutes per side, until brown and crusty on both sides. Transfer to a plate.

Reduce the heat to medium-low, add the remaining 1 tablespoon of oil to the drippings in the pan. Add the Brussels sprouts, season with salt and pepper, and cook, stirring occasionally, for 8 to 10 minutes, until they start to look brown and crusty. Transfer to the same plate with the chicken.

Increase the heat to medium and add the salad dressing, chicken stock concentrate, and 1 cup of water. Season lightly with salt and pepper and allow the pan sauce to simmer and reduce for 5 minutes, scraping up any bits on the bottom of the pan.

Preheat the broiler and adjust the rack to the middle position.

Slide the chicken and Brussels sprouts back into the pan, tossing to ensure everything is coated in the sauce. Broil for 4 to 5 minutes, until the chicken is golden brown and slightly crusty on top (the sugars in the salad dressing will help this happen). Remove from the oven, top with the pecan crumble, and serve right away.

Mediterranean Chicken Meatball Flatbreads with Feta Sauce

Ground chicken and ground turkey have so much potential for greatness, but this potential tends to get lost a lot, making wrong turns and missteps into dry and bland territories that are not great. But! These meatballs benefit from the help of a very effective trick of mine that not only serves to boost their flavor, but also ensures we end up with juicy—very un-dry—meatballs. We'll call upon the help of some crispy french-fried onions, just as we do in my favorite Easiest Hands-Off Spaghetti and Meatballs (page 158), and these meatballs also get a Mediterranean spin thanks to some Italian olive salad (or a similar mix). The olives, garlic, and flavorful oil in these products lend such a helping hand to the lean ground meats that they're so worth seeking out and keeping on hand for meat loaves, burgers, ground meat sauces, and in this case, incredibly tasty meatballs.

SERVES 4

APPROXIMATE TIME: 35 MINUTES

1 pound ground chicken or turkey

½ cup crushed crispy fried onions (like the green bean casserole kind)

⅔ cup chopped Italian olive salad, muffuletta spread, or olive bruschetta (see Note for other subs)

Freshly ground black pepper

8 ounces store-bought tzatziki (Greek cucumber and yogurt dip)

4 ounces crumbled feta

4 flatbreads, such as pita or naan, warmed

Serving suggestions: thinly sliced red onion, fresh sliced tomato, fresh dill, or Friendly Herb Salad, Mediterranean version (page 86)

Adjust an oven rack in the middle position, and preheat to 400 degrees F. Line a baking sheet with parchment paper (this makes for a faster cleanup).

In a bowl, combine the ground chicken, crushed fried onions, and the olive salad. Season with pepper and gently mix just until everything is evenly combined (they shouldn't need salt, as the onions and olives are quite salty, as is the feta).

Roll the mixture into 16 equal-size meatballs, around 1½ inches in diameter. Arrange the meatballs on the baking sheet and bake for 25 minutes. (The olive oil in the mix will likely cause them to spit and sputter, making the oven a cleaner/better/easier cooking option than the stove. A large sheet of aluminum foil laid over the top of the meatballs will catch and prevent some of this splatter, if you like.)

Meanwhile, combine the tzatziki and feta in a small bowl.

You can serve these however you like, but I like to spread some feta sauce onto a warm flatbread and top with several meatballs, slices of red onion and tomato, and a little bit of fresh dill.

Note: Olive spreads like those listed above are great hacks for ensuring you get moist, flavorful meatballs when working with ground turkey or chicken, with one single ingredient. These items are pretty widely available, but if you can't find something that fits the bill, you can substitute ⅔ cup finely chopped green olives (with the pimientos) and 1 tablespoon of olive oil or ⅔ cup processed Italian giardiniera (pickled vegetables, drained).

Beef and Pork

Giardiniera Roasted Pork Sandwich Skillet (with Garlic Mayo)

Like the Mariah Carey of sandwiching, this one just hits all the notes. We've got gooey, crunchy, tangy, salty, herby, creamy, garlicky, and even spicy if you want it. You don't necessarily **have** to serve this sandwich-style, but I love to pile the juicy pork medallions and pickled veggies onto some toasted ciabatta rolls slathered in garlic mayo, and then place the pan right on the table, for dunking. But, that's just me. You do you, here. A jar of briny, pickled Italian- (or Chicago-) style vegetables—known as giardiniera—can save the day when you need a quick, flavorful meal in a hurry. From marinades and omelet toppings to salsas, stews, and sandwiches, this is just an absolute workhorse ingredient that is practically begging to be plucked from the store shelf and allowed to do its thing, making most recipes just a little bit more magical.

SERVES 4

APPROXIMATE TIME: 20 MINUTES

2 tablespoons olive oil, plus extra for drizzling

2 tablespoons butter

1 pound pork tenderloin, sliced into ¼-inch-thick medallions

Salt

Freshly ground black pepper

1 tablespoon Italian seasoning

1 (16-ounce) jar mild giardiniera (crunchy pickled vegetables)

5 to 6 slices provolone cheese or 2 to 3 cups shredded

1 cup mayo

1½ to 2 teaspoons garlic powder

4 ciabatta rolls, split and toasted

Additional topping suggestions: arugula, thinly sliced shallots or scallions

Preheat the broiler to the high setting and adjust the oven rack to the top position.

Heat 1 tablespoon of the oil and 1 tablespoon of the butter in a large skillet over medium-high heat. When the butter is melted, season the pork medallions with salt and pepper and, working in two batches, add them to the pan. Add half of the Italian seasoning per batch and brown the pork on both sides, 3 to 4 minutes per side, adding the remaining 1 tablespoon of oil and 1 tablespoon of butter to the skillet in between batches.

Combine all the pork and any collected juices back into the pan. Add the giardiniera to the skillet, along with ½ cup of liquid from the jar. Spread it all around the pork, and top everything with the cheese. Place under the broiler for 1 to 2 minutes, just until the cheese is melted and bubbling (keep an eye on it!).

Combine the mayo and garlic powder in a small bowl. Spread the mixture onto each of the cut sides of the rolls.

Top the skillet with a scattering of fresh arugula and sliced shallots, if you like. Serve the pork skillet with the toasted ciabatta rolls, so people can make sandwiches, piling the contents onto the bread and saving the pan juices for dredging and dunking (the very best part).

Gooey Pulled Pork and Apple Sliders with "Everything Butter"

Hawaiian Rolls. Store-bought pulled pork. Sliced sweet apples. Gooey, melty white cheddar cheese. These are the building blocks of some seriously addictive, crowd-pleasing sliders. We love this, always. The flavor combination is a play on two classic pairs: pork and apples, and apples and cheddar cheese. Bringing them together under one bun just makes sense, and that final slathering of salty "Everything Butter?" A home run every time.

MAKES 12 SLIDERS

APPROXIMATE TIME: 30 MINUTES

12 Hawaiian rolls

4 tablespoons butter

1 teaspoon everything bagel seasoning

1 (16-ounce) container BBQ pulled pork (see Note)

3 tablespoons soy sauce

Freshly ground black pepper

1 Granny Smith apple, thinly sliced

3 to 4 slices white cheddar cheese, quartered

24 pickled jalapeño slices or dill pickles (you choose!)

Note: If your store doesn't carry pulled pork of any kind, chopped rotisserie chicken, seasoned with your favorite BBQ sauce, is a perfect swap.

Adjust the oven rack to the middle position, and preheat to 375 degrees F.

Set the rolls on a flat surface and, using a large knife, split them crossways in one big cut (sawing helps). Keeping them connected if you can, put the bottoms in a large baking dish.

Combine the butter and everything seasoning in a small saucepan over medium-low heat and cook until the butter has fully melted. Allow it to continue simmering for another couple of minutes, until it appears golden brown, has quieted down, and smells nutty.

Combine the pulled pork with the soy sauce and some black pepper to taste. Top each roll with a couple tablespoons of the pork, followed by a couple slices of apple, a piece (or two) of cheese, and a couple of pickled jalapeños or dill pickles. Put the tops on and spoon/spread some of the brown butter all over, being sure to include the seeds/solid bits. You may not use it all.

Cover with aluminum foil and bake for 15 minutes. Remove the foil and bake for 5 minutes more, or until the cheese is melted and the tops are golden.

Broiled Honey-Soy Pork Lettuce Wraps with Mango

This, the second of two wraps included in this book, is a quick-fix that packs a ton of flavor into a relatively small amount of ingredients. The thing about recipes like this is that you can add many, many more ingredients to the marinade—to the sauce—if you so choose. But honestly? The reaction I received when I served these wraps in their most basic iteration to a room of hungry people was about as positive as I could have hoped for. The honey-soy mixture is essentially a very fast way to approximate a Japanese-style teriyaki sauce, and it brings all the sweet and salty flavor that we need. The marinade will enjoy a happy afterlife as well, as we'll stir it into some creamy mayo, creating a truly addictive sauce that is great on just about anything. Mango and pineapple are both lovely here, seeing as how pork and fruit are a classic pairing. So, just use what you have, love, or looks good at the store.

SERVES 4

APPROXIMATE TIME: < 45 MINUTES

1 (1¼- to 1½-pound) pork
  tenderloin

½ cup soy sauce

½ cup honey

⅔ cup mayonnaise, or more as
  needed

1 teaspoon garlic powder

1 fresh mango, peeled and
  diced or 1½ cups diced
  pineapple

1 head butter lettuce or Boston
  leaf lettuce, whole leaves
  separated

Cut the pork tenderloin against the grain into thin strips and transfer them to a bowl or large resealable plastic bag.

Combine the soy sauce and honey in a small bowl and pour half the mixture over the pork. Set aside to marinate at room temperature for 30 minutes.

Meanwhile, whisk the mayo into the remaining honey-soy mixture until smooth. Add the garlic powder and mix well. You can add as much mayo as you like to this, if you'd like a thicker sauce.

Adjust an oven rack to the top position, and preheat the broiler to high.

Discard the marinade and pat the pork dry. Arrange the pork on a baking sheet in a single layer and broil for 5 minutes. Carefully and evenly scatter over the mango and broil for 2 to 3 minutes, until the pork is just cooked through and nicely charred on the tops. (If parts of the pork are charring faster than you'd like, you can lay a piece of aluminum foil over top to slow that down.)

Serve the broiled pork and fruit in the lettuce leaves, doubling up the leaves for extra durability. Drizzle with the creamy honey-soy sauce.

Easiest Hands-Off Spaghetti and Meatballs

This is one of the fastest, easiest ways to enjoy spaghetti and meatballs that I know. By cooking the noodles right in the sauce in the baking dish, you get a brilliant one-pan meal that will make everyone smile when you set it on the table. Juicy, flavorful meatballs get a fast-tracked boost from both store-bought pesto and a favorite meatball/meatloaf hack of mine—french-fried onions. You get the aromatic flavor from the onions and the breadcrumb effect from the crispy coating. Two birds, one stone, right? But the greatest part of this recipe is how the rendered drippings from the roasting meatballs flavor the (jarred) tomato sauce so brilliantly, standing in for the butter I'd typically use. These meatballs come together in a snap, baking right along with the noodles in this cozy, easy-as-pie dinner. If you want to make it even faster, just use the fresh prepared meatballs from your grocery store's meat department.

SERVES 4

APPROXIMATE TIME: 45 MINUTES

12 ounces spaghetti, broken in half

1 (32-ounce) jar good-quality marinara sauce

1 pound ground beef

1 cup crushed french-fried onions

½ cup basil pesto (Rana brand is excellent)

½ teaspoon salt

Freshly ground black pepper

Serving suggestions: fresh chopped basil, olive oil for drizzling, grated Parmesan

Adjust the oven rack to the middle position, and preheat to 425 degrees F. Spray a 9 x 13-inch baking dish with nonstick spray or grease with butter.

Spread out the spaghetti in the dish and cover with the sauce. Add 2 cups of water and toss to ensure the pasta is coated.

In a large bowl, combine the beef, crushed onions, and pesto and season with the salt and some pepper. Mix just until evenly combined. Don't overwork! Roll the meat mixture into balls, 1 to 1½ inches in size. You should get about 15 to 16 meatballs. Place these meatballs on top of the pasta in the dish, cover with aluminum foil, and bake for 30 minutes.

Remove the foil and give the pasta a good stir all over (tongs are great for this), loosening it and mixing it gently. Bake 5 to 7 minutes more, uncovered, until the pasta is cooked through. You can add an extra splash of water to the dish if it seems a bit drier than you'd prefer.

Serve with fresh basil, a drizzle of olive oil, and a shower of grated Parmesan on top.

Malaysian Black Pepper Braised Beef Lettuce Wraps

SERVES 4 TO 6

APPROXIMATE TIME: 3 HOURS (2½ HOURS HANDS OFF)

1 cup sweetened coconut flakes

½ yellow onion, coarsely chopped

4 garlic cloves

1 to 2 red chile peppers, seeded

4 ounces Thai-style red curry paste

1 tablespoon ginger paste or 1-inch knob fresh peeled ginger, minced

1 tablespoon fish sauce

2 tablespoons vegetable oil, plus more as needed

2 pounds cubed stew beef

Salt

Freshly ground black pepper

1 (15-ounce) can coconut milk

1 cup low-sodium beef broth

¼ cup soy sauce

Butter lettuce, whole leaves separated, for serving

Serving suggestions: shredded carrot, sliced scallions, cucumbers, sesame seeds, toasted coconut, cilantro

A nod to one of the world's most delicious beef recipes, beef rendang, this recipe is a true powerhouse. It is so utterly delicious, it has the ability to summon people (neighbors, mail carriers, etc.) from the streets (this is actually true). It smells incredible and you just know something magical is happening in the kitchen. I have trouble procuring the ingredients for the traditional Malay-style dish, so I've created a recipe that is something of an homage to the real thing, but also doable for my weekly meal rotation and budget. An alluring combination of ginger, garlic, toasted coconut, soy sauce, and red curry paste goes to serious work on some simple cubes of stew beef. I like to serve this lettuce wrap style, as the fresh lettuce balances the rich meat beautifully, but rice or even rice noodles would work just as well.

Put the coconut in a large, dry Dutch oven or ovenproof pot over medium heat. Stirring occasionally, toast the coconut just until it's golden brown and smells nutty and sweet. Transfer the coconut to a food processor along with the onion, garlic, chiles, curry paste, ginger paste, and fish sauce. Process until smooth.

Increase the heat under the pot to high and add the oil. When it's shimmering hot, add the beef, season with salt and pepper, and brown it all over (it doesn't have to get super dark here), about 5 minutes.

Add the curry paste mixture to the pot, and cook for a couple of minutes, stirring. Add the coconut milk, broth, and soy sauce and stir well. Put the lid on the pot and braise for 2½ hours, until the meat is easily shredded, and fall-apart tender.

Serve the beef, shredded or not, in the lettuce "cups" (I usually stack two lettuce leaves together, for extra durability.). Top with any or all of the following: shredded carrot, scallions, cucumbers, sesame seeds, toasted coconut, and/or cilantro.

A Shepherd's Cottage Pie

For this recipe to technically be deserving of the title "shepherd's pie," it needs to be made with lamb. So, seeing as how I've written it to work with either ground lamb or ground beef (called a "cottage pie"), we're mashing up the two names into one inclusive moniker that lets us choose our own savory meat pie adventure. Speaking of mashing up, this is one of three instant mashed potato appearances in this book (see also A Mashed Potato Revival on page 115 and the Seared Scallops and Gnocchi with Pesto Cream Sauce on page 175) and a pie such as this is the perfect time to lean on a store-bought mashed potato. We'll doctor them up with some cheese and butter, growing the flavor a bit, and then slather them on top of a very simple (hello, frozen vegetables) filling. This is cozy, soul-warming fare that is made all the more comforting by the ease with which it is prepared. I just love this for us.

SERVES 4

APPROXIMATE TIME: < 1 HOUR

1 (32-ounce) container prepared mashed potatoes

3 tablespoons butter

⅔ cup shredded sharp cheddar cheese, or as needed, plus extra for topping

Salt

Freshly ground black pepper

3 tablespoons olive oil, divided, plus more as needed

1 pound ground beef or lamb

1 small yellow onion, diced

1 (10-ounce) bag frozen peas and carrots

1 teaspoon garlic powder

2 teaspoons curry powder

2 teaspoons poultry seasoning or Italian seasoning

2 tablespoons tomato paste

2 tablespoons all-purpose flour

1 cup stock (beef, veggie, or chicken are all fine)

Topping suggestion: minced fresh chives

Adjust the oven rack to the middle position, and preheat to 400 degrees F.

Put the mashed potatoes in a small-to-medium pot over medium-low heat, along with the butter and cheese. Cook until both the butter and cheese are melted. Taste and season with salt and pepper.

Heat 2 tablespoons of the oil in a large ovenproof skillet over medium heat. When it's shimmering hot, add the meat in a single layer, giving it as much surface area to brown as you can. Season with salt and pepper and leave it alone for at least 5 minutes, allowing it to get really brown. Stir, and brown the other side for a minute or so. Transfer the meat to a plate, leaving the drippings in the skillet.

Add the remaining tablespoon of oil to the pan and, still over medium heat, add the onion, frozen veggies, garlic powder, curry powder, poultry seasoning, and tomato paste. Stir, allowing the veggies to thaw and the flavors to mesh, for about 5 minutes.

Sprinkle the flour over top and, stirring, let it cook for about 1 minute. Add the stock and bring the mixture to a simmer, stirring to combine.

Add the meat back into the pan, stir to combine, and then smooth the potatoes across the top. Sprinkle with any extra cheese, if you like, and bake for 35 to 40 minutes, or until golden brown on top. Garnish with minced chives if you like and serve.

Chocolate-Chile Pork Shoulder with Beans

So yes, this is a play on the whole pork-and-beans concept, of which I'm a huge fan. Pans of basic baked beans have frankly never done much for me, as they're often too sweet and one-note-tasting to be of much interest. But when they slow-roast in the salty, spicy renderings of a big piece of rich pork shoulder? Forget about it. The sweetness lifts up the richness of the menacingly dark-crusted pork (hello, cocoa), working in tandem with that spicy pepper to create a finished dish that is definitely not one-note. Topped with fresh herbs and sharp red onion, this is best enjoyed with some warmed tortillas or flatbread to help grab and drag every dripping, delicious bite.

MAKES 4 SERVINGS

APPROXIMATE TIME: 3 HOURS 45
   MINUTES, ALMOST ENTIRELY
   HANDS-OFF

4½ to 5 pounds boneless pork shoulder

2 teaspoons salt, plus more as needed

Freshly ground black pepper

2 chipotle peppers, minced plus 2 teaspoons adobo sauce from the can

2 teaspoons garlic powder

1 tablespoon unsweetened cocoa powder

Juice of 1 lime

1 (28-ounce) can baked beans, drained but not rinsed

½ red onion, sliced

Coarsely chopped cilantro or Simple Arugula Salad (page 86)

Warmed flour or corn tortillas, for serving

Serving suggestion: an everyday red slaw (see Note)

Adjust the oven rack to the middle position, and preheat to 325 degrees F.

Place the pork in a large lidded pot and season lightly with some salt and pepper. In a small bowl, combine the minced chipotles, adobo sauce, garlic powder, cocoa powder, lime juice, and the 2 teaspoons of salt (this is a lot of pork, so it needs a lot of salt). Stir to combine and rub this paste all over the surface of the pork. Pour the beans all around the pork and add 1 cup water. Season the beans with salt and pepper and stir to mix a bit.

Put the lid on and bake for 3 hours. Increase the temperature to 425 degrees F, take the lid off, and cook for another 40 to 45 minutes, or until the pork is incredibly tender and easily sliced or shredded.

Before serving, I like to take a few minutes to skim some of the fat off the top of the beans. This is a rich dish by design, but there will be excess rendered fat, which can be saved and used for frying up some eggs in the morning, or not as you prefer.

Serve the pork with the beans on the side, topped with some sliced red onion, cilantro, warmed tortillas, and, if you like, the red cabbage slaw (see Note).

Note: I love to serve this with a very simple red cabbage slaw, for crunch and to balance the richness of the pork. Combine 3 to 4 cups of finely shredded red cabbage with enough mayo to fully moisten. Add a handful of chopped cilantro (optional), the whites and greens of 3 chopped scallions, the juice of 1 lime, and some salt and pepper to taste.

Naan Cuban Sandwiches

A cross-section of these sandwiches reads like a deliciously stratified greatest hits list of my most-loved, most frequently enjoyed foods. I always have pork tenderloin in my fridge, as well as some good-quality store-bought naan (Indian flatbread), pickles, deli meat, mustard, and sliced cheese. My family's deep affection for sandwiches accounts for much of this, and the day I realized that these things could provide a very delicious take on one of the world's great sandwiches—it was game on. Traditionally, the Cuban sandwich is made with roasted pork that has been flavored with mojo, a citrusy, garlicky marinade that is otherworldly delicious. To hasten the process a bit, and make it a quick meal, I simply season and roast a pork tenderloin instead of a larger cut. Also, to preserve that garlicky, aromatic flavor we're missing from the mojo, a store-bought garlic naan makes a fine substitution for the Cuban bread. To make this even faster, you can: 1) Procure some pre-roasted pork from your store—carnitas or unsauced pulled pork is great. 2) Bake the assembled sandwiches in a 400 degree F oven until toasted and gooey, skipping the skillet altogether.

MAKES 4 SANDWICHES
APPROXIMATE TIME: 40 MINUTES

1 (1- to 1¼-pound) pork tenderloin

2 teaspoons lemon pepper

1½ teaspoons salt

1 to 2 teaspoons ground cumin

8 pieces toasted garlic naan

Mayonnaise, for spreading (optional)

12 to 16 slices ham

16 to 20 dill pickle chips

8 slices Swiss cheese

Yellow mustard

Olive oil and/or butter, for cooking

Adjust the oven rack to the middle position, and preheat to 400 degrees F. Line a baking sheet with aluminum foil.

Place the pork on the baking sheet and season with the lemon pepper, salt, and cumin, ensuring it is evenly coated. Roast for 25 to 27 minutes, or until just barely pink in the center (it will continue cooking). Wrap the pork in the foil and let it "carryover cook" on the counter for 5 to 10 minutes so the juices can settle and disperse.

Thinly slice the pork. To make the sandwiches, spread some mayo on the back sides of 4 naan slices. Top each of those with a couple slices of ham, some pickles, some sliced pork, some Swiss cheese, and yellow mustard to taste. Top with the remaining naan slices.

Heat a couple tablespoons of either olive oil or butter (or a combo of both) in a large skillet set over medium-high heat. Working in batches as needed, cook the sandwiches for a couple of minutes per side, until the naan is golden brown and the cheese has melted. Pressing down on the sandwiches as they cook helps create an extra-crispy crust. Alternatively, you can put all of the sandwiches on a baking sheet (I opt for the same pan I used to roast the pork) and bake them at 400 degrees F for 8 to 10 minutes.

Spaghetti with Sausage and Peppers Ragù

SERVES 4 TO 6

APPROXIMATE TIME: 30 MINUTES

2 tablespoons olive oil

1 pound sweet Italian sausage

8 ounces mini sweet peppers, trimmed, seeded, and coarsely chopped

2 celery stalks, coarsely chopped

2 carrots, chopped (no need to peel)

1 small onion, quartered

2 teaspoons chicken or beef stock concentrate (I like Better Than Bouillon)

6 ounces tomato paste

Salt

Freshly ground black pepper

1 (14.5-ounce) can crushed tomatoes

½ cup grated Parmesan cheese, plus more for topping

¾ pound spaghetti, or any long noodle you like

Serving suggestion: fresh basil

My favorite thing about this recipe is the fact that the sauce has just as much—if not more—veggies going on as it does meat. Loads of celery, carrot, onion, and sweet baby peppers combine in a vibrant, vegetal mélange that does a lot of light-but-heavy lifting in what is otherwise a sausage sauce. Yes, we're going to bypass a lot of time and steps in a traditional Bolognese-style sauce by using flavorful Italian sausage instead. This single move helps make this a 30-minute meal that packs tremendous punch in every bite. Rather than keeping the veggies in large chunks or strips, I like to blend them into a pulp. This serves to draw out their inherent moisture and colors, creating a beautifully flavorful and memorable ragù—my go-to ragù, in fact.

Heat the oil in a large skillet over medium-high heat. When it's hot, add the sausage, breaking it up and spreading it out in a big layer. Let the sausage cook for about 5 minutes, until it's very browned and crusty on the bottom.

Meanwhile, combine the peppers, celery, carrots, and onion in a food processor and pulse until you have a smooth-ish pulp.

When the sausage has browned, add the veggie pulp to the pan, along with the stock concentrate, and tomato paste. Season with salt and pepper. Cook for about 5 minutes more.

Add the crushed tomatoes and ½ cup grated Parmesan cheese. Let the ragù simmer over low heat while you cook the pasta to al dente in salted water according to package directions. Transfer the cooked, drained pasta directly into the skillet with the sauce and toss well to coat. Serve with fresh basil, and extra Parmesan, if you like.

The Ugly Dumpling

There may be a no more beloved food item in my house than beautiful Chinese-style dumplings. My son Easton has classically been a picky eater, but he has never turned down a dumpling of any sort. This recipe grew from that love, and also my own innate laziness when it comes to making individual dumplings, as I don't have the skills or patience to do them much justice. So, I am honoring the pros here, tipping my imaginary chef's toque in their delicious direction. Rather than stuffing this immensely flavorful meat filling into dumpling wrappers, I toss it with noodles, allowing the rich sauce to coat every strand, making for one slurpably satisfying dumpling-noodle marriage of sorts.

SERVES 4

APPROXIMATE TIME: < 25 MINUTES

2 tablespoons vegetable or canola oil

1 pound ground pork or beef

2 tablespoons oyster sauce

⅓ cup soy sauce

1 teaspoon sesame oil

½ cup Shaoxing wine or dry sherry

4 garlic cloves, minced

1-inch knob fresh ginger, peeled and grated or minced or 1 tablespoon ginger paste

1 bunch scallions, chopped, both white and green parts

¾ pound long noodles (any kind you like or have around)

Salt

Serving suggestions: Friendly Herb Salad, Southeast Asian edition (page 86), or chopped cilantro, fresh torn Thai basil or basil, chopped scallion greens, and cut limes for squeezing

Heat the oil in a large skillet over medium-high heat. When it's hot, add the meat, spreading it out as best you can across the pan. Let it brown for 6 to 8 minutes before moving it (resist the urge!).

Meanwhile, combine the oyster sauce, soy sauce, sesame oil, wine, garlic, and ginger. When the meat is very browned, stir it and add the scallion whites. Cook for about 30 seconds and add the sauce. Reduce the heat to medium-low and let the pan simmer gently, stirring often, for a few minutes to thicken the sauce a bit.

Prepare the noodles according to package directions in salted water, reserving ¾ cup of the starchy cooking liquid just before draining. (If using rice noodles, be sure to drain them, rinse them, and then drain again.)

Toss the noodles in the "dumpling" meat sauce and taste for seasoning, adding more of anything you like (I often find it needs a pinch of salt and a splash of the reserved noodle cooking water). Serve with the scallion greens, fresh limes for squeezing, and some chopped cilantro, if desired.

Note: Shaoxing wine can be tough to locate, and I've found that a dry cooking sherry stands in really well for this recipe.

Bruschetta Smash Burgers

Roll up your sleeves, prop your elbows up just a little higher, and get ready for a juicy, drippy, utterly satisfying burger experience. I've read that in Mexico, once one commences eating a taco, they typically try to finish it without putting it down. There is no starting and stopping, as the inherent messiness from all the delicious salsas, meats, and fillings requires a one-fell-swoop style of eating. This, incidentally, very much applies to my burgers here. They are very juicy thanks to the bruschetta, which is an Italian tomato salsa that adds tremendous flavor to these quick and easy burgers. To hasten the whole process and usher in a good helping of homemade-ish ease, we'll put a package of store-bought meatballs to good use, transforming them into flavorful burgers instead. Often sold in packages of 12 (usually about 1½ inches in size), I find that by smashing three meatballs together you can create a perfect burger, primed for optimal crisping and browning when pressed into a screaming hot, olive oil-slicked pan.

SERVES 4

APPROXIMATE TIME: < 20 MINUTES

1 cup mayonnaise

1 tablespoon store-bought basil pesto

1 tablespoon olive oil, plus more as needed

12 store-bought premade meatballs (raw, not frozen)

Salt

Freshly ground black pepper

8 ounces sliced fresh mozzarella cheese

8 to 10 tablespoons store-bought bruschetta (see Note)

1 cup baby arugula

4 ciabatta rolls or the burger buns of your choice, toasted

Combine the mayo and pesto in a small bowl and set aside.

Heat about 1 tablespoon of olive oil in a large nonstick or cast-iron skillet (or flattop/griddle) over high heat. Combine the meatballs into 4 larger meatballs (each consisting of 3 smaller meatballs).

When the skillet is very hot, working in batches and adding more oil as needed, smash the meatballs into the hot pan, creating large thin patties. Season lightly with salt and pepper. Cook for 3 to 3½ minutes until very browned on the first side. Flip the burgers, top with mozzarella, and put a lid over the pan. Continue cooking for 2 to 3 minutes more, until the burgers are cooked through and the cheese is melted.

To build the burgers, slather the cut sides of all the ciabatta rolls with some of the pesto mayo. Place a cooked burger on each of the 4 bun bottoms and top with a couple of tablespoons of bruschetta. Top with some arugula and the bun tops.

Notes: If you are unable to find premade bruschetta, you can quickly make your own by stirring together 1 cup chopped fresh tomatoes, ¼ to ⅓ cup chopped white onion, 1 to 2 tablespoons freshly chopped basil leaves, 1 to 2 tablespoons olive oil, 1 freshly grated garlic clove, and some salt and pepper to taste.

Store-bought bruschetta also makes one of the greatest pasta sauces you'll ever try. Tossing hot noodles with the raw, olive oil–rich salsa and serving it up with big pieces of torn burrata cheese is one of the nicest summertime meals I know.

Sicilian Seared Steaks on Toast

Bistecca alla Siciliana—Sicilian-style steak—is typically marinated in garlic and olive oil and then crusted in Parmesan cheese and breadcrumbs, creating a fetching, crispy browned crust when all is said and done. A definite nod to that classic preparation, my version here skips that breading step and opts instead to pile the steak on top of some deeply toasted Italian bread slices, showering everything in nutty Parmesan cheese. Same components, different arrangement. A good-quality store-bought pesto stands as the anchoring bed for this hearty collective of simple things, its herby, cheesy, and garlicky flavors helping get us to that Sicilian state of mind in a hurry. Oh, cara mia . . .

SERVES 4

APPROXIMATE TIME: 15 MINUTES

1½ to 2 pounds sirloin steak(s)

Salt

Freshly ground black pepper

1 tablespoon cooking oil, plus more as needed

⅓ cup store-bought basil pesto

4 thick slices Italian bread or bread of your choice, deeply toasted

2 to 3 cups baby arugula

Freshly shaved Parmesan cheese, for topping

⅓ cup toasted pine nuts (see Note)

Optional Precook Step: 30 minutes before cooking, season your steaks generously with salt and pepper on both sides and place on a plate, uncovered, on the countertop to air dry and season (this gives the very best crust).

Preheat a skillet or grill pan (preferably cast iron, if you've got it) over medium-high to high heat and turn on your exhaust fan and get a splatter screen ready, if you have one. Add 1 tablespoon of cooking oil to the pan. Sear the steaks for about 4 minutes, until deeply, fantastically browned on both sides, for medium-rare. You can continue to cook the steaks on the stovetop to achieve your preferred doneness level or place the pan in a 400 degree F oven for about 5 minutes to cook them further.

Let the cooked steaks rest for 10 minutes before slicing thinly.

To serve, slather some pesto all over a big serving platter, using as much as you like (or you can do this on individual plates). Arrange the toasts on top. Lay the steak slices on top of the toast and top with some arugula and shaved Parmesan. If using, scatter some toasted pine nuts over top and serve.

Note: To toast pine nuts, cook them in a small skillet over medium heat and, stirring occasionally, let them gradually toast for 3 to 4 minutes, until you can smell them and they begin to pick up a little color (it goes fast!).

Fish and Seafood

Seared Scallops and Gnocchi with Pesto Cream Sauce

I used to say that gnocchi weren't worth the fuss, that it was exclusively a restaurant sort of dish. I mean, what with the peeling and cooking of the potatoes, the shredding of them only to realize that we've barely even begun to "gnocchi" yet . . . yeah, that never quite did it for me. Until I found a hack that changed the whole game. Using instant mashed potatoes cuts that portion of the program out, allowing us to still make pillowy soft "homemade-ish" gnocchi in about 10 minutes. To make things even more alluring, we'll sear some beautiful sea scallops and pile them on top. A two-minute sauce made from the salty, buttery pan drippings, a dollop of crème fraîche, and some (store-bought) pesto seal the whole decadent deal.

SERVES 4

APPROXIMATE TIME: < 30 MINUTES

1 cup all-purpose flour, plus extra for dusting

1 egg

16 ounces prepared mashed potatoes

½ teaspoon salt, plus more as needed

Freshly ground black pepper

2 tablespoons butter

2 tablespoons olive oil

1 pound jumbo wild sea scallops, thawed if frozen (see Note)

¾ cup frozen green peas

2 tablespoons pesto

2 tablespoons crème fraîche or sour cream

Serving suggestion: flaky sea salt for sprinkling

Pour the flour in a large bowl and create a well in the middle. Crack the egg into the well and add the mashed potatoes. Season with the salt and as much pepper as you like. Using a fork, stir the flour into the eggs and potatoes, until everything is well combined.

Dust a clean work surface with a little flour. Divide the gnocchi dough into four pieces and roll each into a long rope about ¾ inch thick. Using the fork, cut the ropes into ¾-inch pieces. Using that very same fork, gently press into the pieces and roll them along the tines of the fork, creating lovely grooves. Gently squeeze each gnocchi a bit, plumping them back up.

Bring a pot of salted water to a boil. Working in batches, boil the gnocchi for about 45 seconds. They'll bob up to the surface when they're technically done, and I like to let them swim a little longer to puff a bit more. Using a slotted spoon or strainer, gently transfer the gnocchi to a plate or tray. Reserve about ½ cup of the gnocchi water.

Heat the butter and oil in a large skillet over medium heat. Pat the scallops dry and season them with salt and pepper. Working in a couple of batches, sear the scallops for about 3 minutes per side, until golden brown. Transfer them to a plate while you make the 2-minute sauce.

Keeping the buttery drippings in the pan and the heat still on medium, add the gnocchi and peas to the skillet. Add the pesto and crème fraîche and toss and stir to combine everything. You can add a little of the reserved gnocchi water, if needed. Pour the saucy gnocchi and peas onto a big platter or onto individual plates. Top with the scallops and serve with flaky sea salt for sprinkling, if desired.

Note: Sometimes scallops come with what is called a "foot" attached to their sides. Not actually a foot at all, these little flaps are bits of muscle that are totally edible but tougher than the rest of the scallop. To remove, just pull them off.

Lowcountry Boil–Stuffed Sweet Potatoes with Herby Old Bay Butter

A salty-skinned, roasted-to-death sweet potato is a great thing all by itself. Rarely do I feel compelled to stuff mine with much beyond some salted maple butter, or maybe some hot honey and sour cream, but this particular hodgepodge of things has shifted my gaze for sure. While I will be living in Portland, Oregon, when this book comes out, I am writing these recipes from my kitchen in Charleston, South Carolina. So, my flavor choices are inspired by Southern *and* Pacific Northwestern coastal waters to be sure. In this case, the beloved Southern crawfish boil was on my mind as I tested flavorful potato toppers. Crawfish isn't exactly easy to find, so I reach for large shrimp instead. Smoked sausage and sweet corn kernels round out the scene and are set off by a dollop of Old Bay butter. Simple, fast, and so-very-flavorful, this is one I've made more times than I can count.

SERVES 4

APPROXIMATE TIME: 1½ HOURS
  (MOSTLY HANDS-OFF)

4 sweet potatoes, scrubbed and dried

Vegetable oil, for coating the potatoes and shrimp

Salt

Freshly ground black pepper

12 to 14 ounces smoked sausage links, cut into bite-size pieces

1 pound large uncooked shrimp, peeled and deveined

1 (10-ounce) bag frozen corn

8 tablespoons butter, at room temperature

1 teaspoon Old Bay seasoning

Serving suggestion: chopped fresh green herbs

Adjust one oven rack to the top third position and another to the middle position and preheat to 425 degrees F. For easier cleanup, cover a large baking sheet with aluminum foil.

Place the potatoes on the baking sheet and prick them all over with a fork several times. Coat each potato all over with oil. Season generously with salt and pepper. Roast the potatoes directly on the middle rack for 70 to 75 minutes or until very tender (if I have time, I often leave them in the oven, heat off, to continue softening and collapsing, but that's optional). Place the baking sheet on the lowest rack, or even the oven floor, to catch any oil drippings.

When the potatoes have 30 minutes of baking time remaining, put the sausage pieces on one half of a second baking sheet. Roast them for 10 minutes on the top rack. Take the pan out and add the shrimp to the other half. Drizzle the shrimp lightly with oil and season with salt and pepper. Scatter the corn all over top of everything and put back in the oven to roast for 7 to 9 minutes more, until the shrimp is just done (pink and curled).

Combine the butter and Old Bay seasoning in a small bowl (you can add more to taste). Season with salt and pepper to taste.

Let the potatoes cool for a few minutes, until easily handled, and split them lengthwise down the middle, taking care not to cut all the way through. Fill the potatoes with the corn, sausage, and shrimp mixture and serve with fresh green herbs and the Old Bay butter.

Not a Piccata

MAKES 4 SERVINGS

APPROXIMATE TIME: < 30 MINUTES

4 (5- to 7-ounce) skinless fish fillets, such as salmon, cod, grouper, tilapia, or flounder

Salt

Freshly ground black pepper

4 tablespoons butter

3 tablespoons olive oil

½ small red onion, sliced, divided

3 to 4 tablespoons capers, drained (just use as many as you like)

½ lemon, thinly sliced, seeds removed

Zest of 1 navel orange

Friendly Herb Salad, Mediterranean version (page 86), or fresh dill

1 tablespoon sesame seeds (optional)

Serving suggestions: roasted green veggies (since the oven is already on), such as asparagus (pictured) or broccoli

When I think about dinners with my extended family, three things come to mind immediately: Italian sugo simmering away on the stovetop, pimiento cheese, and piccatas, which is one of my favorite food groups (I think we can call it a food group). From chicken and grouper to pork tenderloin and even trout, I think I have "piccata-ed" just about everything. Which is why this recipe is written to account for just that— you can use any skinless fish fillets that you like. Here, we'll remove the breading and pan-frying portion of the piccata program and stick to the simplest, most deliciously effective parts. The addition of a hint of orange to the classic lemon brings a lovely aroma to the rich butter and olive-oil slicked salmon, and capers and red onion are there to punch right back. So simple, so fast, this one is a forever go-to of mine.

Preheat the oven to 350 degrees F.

Place the fish in a baking dish and season with salt and pepper.

Melt the butter in a saucepan over medium heat. Add the olive oil, half of the sliced onion, and the capers. Season lightly with salt and pepper. Simmer gently for 1 to 2 minutes. Pour the mixture over the salmon in the baking dish. Arrange the lemon slices over top and scatter the orange zest evenly over top.

Bake for 11 to 12 minutes, until the fish is just cooked through and opaque in the center (110 to 125 degrees F for medium-rare), depending on the thickness of the fish. You can add 1 minute if you like your fish closer to medium.

I like to plate the fish and break it up a little bit, spooning some of the butter from the baking dish over top, along with some of the cooked onions and capers. Serve with fresh herbs, some of the remaining sliced onion, and a shower of sesame seeds. Add some roasted vegetables and you have a fabulous meal.

Buttery Poached Fish with Fennel and Tomatoes

What a total pinch hitter this one is. Simply elegant and so beautiful, this is one of the greatest back-pocket entertaining recipes I have up my sleeve. I'm sharing it here because it's unbelievably fast, easy, and nearly foolproof to prepare, but I also have noticed that, for many people, both fish *and* fennel tend to come with certain intimidation factors. But this recipe asks almost nothing of you, really, so far as their cooking is concerned. I just want you to give it a go, abandoning any preconceived notions that "you can't cook fish." You absolutely can, and it'll be beautiful. The buttery anise and tomato-scented poaching liquid will do all the work. You just have to lay those cod fillets in the pan, cover it, and then walk away for about 10 minutes. As far as the fennel goes, you can toss or save the tough stems (we're just using the bulb), but be sure to chop up some of the fluffy green fronds to use as a topper for the finished dish.

SERVES 4

APPROXIMATE TIME: < 30 MINUTES

8 tablespoons butter, divided

1 pint cherry tomatoes, halved

1 bulb fennel, thinly sliced or shaved (save the frilly fronds for topping)

Salt

Freshly ground black pepper

4 (6- to 8-ounce) cod fillets

Chopped green herbs, for topping, such as parsley, scallions/chives, dill, fennel fronds

Serving suggestion: crusty bread

Heat 4 tablespoons of butter in a large pan over medium heat. When it's melted, add the tomatoes and fennel, and sauté for 10 to 12 minutes, until the tomatoes have shriveled and burst.

Add ½ cup of water and nestle the fish into the pan, ensuring that they are halfway submerged in the liquid. Season with salt and pepper and dot the whole pan with the remaining 4 tablespoons of butter. Cover the pan and allow the fish to gently poach over medium-low heat for 9 to 10 minutes, until just cooked.

Serve simply, with a shower of freshly chopped herbs (fennel fronds and parsley, pictured), and some crusty bread for sopping.

Roasted Shrimp with Creamy Chili-Garlic Sauce

Taking only about seven minutes from start to finish, this recipe is a regular in my kitchen. There's nothing wrong with a classic shrimp cocktail, but due to some mildly traumatic childhood encounters with overly horseradish-ed cocktail sauce, I tend to steer clear. Instead, I love to serve this version, which only loosely resembles the standard, featuring roasted shrimp and a creamy/spicy/salty dipping sauce that replaces the cocktail variety. Roasting is the very best way to prepare shrimp, in my humble opinion, as it renders incredibly juicy, perfectly cooked results every time. That alone is reason enough to give this recipe a try. You may never look to freezing cold, rubbery shrimp again.

SERVES 4 TO 6 AS A MAIN, SIDE OR
    STARTER
APPROXIMATE TIME: 10 MINUTES

24 ounces large (31 to 40 per pound) uncooked shrimp, peeled and deveined (tails on or off)

2 tablespoons olive oil

Salt

Freshly ground black pepper

½ cup mayonnaise

1 scant tablespoon soy sauce

1 tablespoon Asian-style chili-garlic sauce

Adjust the oven rack to the middle position, and preheat to 400 degrees F.

On a large baking sheet toss the shrimp with the oil and some salt and pepper (about 1 teaspoon of each). Roast for 7 to 8 minutes, until just done (pink and curled).

Meanwhile, in a small bowl, stir together the mayo, soy sauce, and chili-garlic sauce. Pile the shrimp onto a platter and serve with the sauce.

Note: Chili-garlic sauce is found in the Asian or international section of most supermarkets, and is a useful ingredient to keep on hand, offering both heat and a garlicky punch to everything from soups and stews to marinades, rubs, and in this case, quick-flavored sauces and mayos.

Crispy Skin Fish with Feta Rice and Scallion Relish

When I was a kid, I probably played restaurant more than any other form of make-believe. I'd pretend to take reservations over the phone, then would morph from the chef to the maître d' to the diners, all in one seamless dance that I may or may not still dabble in from time to time. This recipe—this gorgeous crispy skin fish number—has the feel of a fancy night out at a special place but is wonderfully simple to pull off. We'll employ some instant rice here, a big time-saving move. But just be sure to grab a high-quality organic brand, as they are usually devoid of unnecessary preservatives. The addition of feta lifts the rice up and into a place far more interesting, and I love to serve these warm, spiced cucumbers as a slightly different approach to this typically chilled veggie.

SERVES 4

APPROXIMATE TIME: 30 MINUTES

1 English cucumber

4 tablespoons olive oil, divided, plus more as needed

2 garlic cloves, minced, divided

1 teaspoon ground cumin, divided

1 teaspoon ground coriander, divided

1 bunch scallions, diced, white and green parts separated, divided

Salt

Freshly ground black pepper

16 to 18 ounces organic instant rice, any variety (such as Seeds of Change)

4 to 6 ounces crumbled feta cheese

Juice and zest of 1 lemon

4 (5- to 7-ounce) skin-on fish fillets such as barramundi, snapper, or salmon

Serving suggestion: fresh lemons, halved, for squeezing

Halve the cucumber lengthwise and cut into 1½-inch pieces. Put them in a sealable plastic bag (a bowl also works, in a pinch).

Heat 2 tablespoons of oil, half the garlic, the cumin, and coriander in a large nonstick skillet over medium heat. Once the garlic just starts to sizzle, pour the flavored oil over the chopped cucumbers. Add ½ of the scallion whites. Season with salt and pepper and toss to coat. Using whatever implement you like, smash the cucumbers lightly, breaking them apart just a little bit (this releases extra juice and flavor). Set aside for now.

Prepare the rice according to package directions, transfer to a bowl, and toss with the feta.

Transfer the remaining scallion whites and half the scallion greens to a bowl and add the lemon juice and zest, the remaining 2 tablespoons olive oil, and the remaining garlic to make a relish. Season with salt and pepper and toss to coat. Taste and adjust as needed.

Add enough olive oil to the skillet to fully coat the pan (no need to wipe it out, unless you want to), and increase the heat to medium-high. Pat the fish dry and season the fish on both sides with salt and pepper. When the oil is shimmering hot, working in batches as needed, lay the fish skin-side down and cook for 4 to 5 minutes without moving, until the skin is crispy. Turn and cook 2 to 3 minutes more, or just until cooked through. Taking the fish off the heat a little early is a great insurance policy against overcooking and dryness . . . just saying.

Serve the fish over the feta rice with the spiced cucumber salad on the side and some scallion relish drizzled over top with some lemon juice.

Shrimp Linguine with Creamy Clam Sauce

The day that I realized you could use a container of (good-quality) New England clam chowder as the base for a sauce was the day my pasta game changed forever. For some reason, though they're incredibly fast and simple to prepare, fresh clams are a tough sell for most home cooks. I only know this because I've been trying to sell them throughout the whole of my decade-long career in public recipe sharing. I'm hoping that this simple chowder hack will get you to serve clams a little more, dip your toes into the water, so to speak. They are just beyond delicious—such special sea-born treasures—and they're pretty iconic when paired with long, tangly noodles. All it takes is a few fresh aromatics to really make this sauce next-level great.

SERVES 4

APPROXIMATE TIME: 45 MINUTES

Olive oil, for cooking

1 to 1¼ pounds medium uncooked shrimp, peeled and deveined, thawed if frozen

1 large beefsteak tomato or 3 Roma tomatoes, chopped

Salt

Freshly ground black pepper

1 small onion, diced

2 stalks celery, diced

2 teaspoons thyme leaves, chopped

2 garlic cloves, minced

1 pound prepared New England clam chowder, thawed if frozen

1 cup grated Parmesan cheese, divided

1 pound linguine

Serving suggestion: chopped basil or parsley

Heat 2 tablespoons of olive oil in a large, deep skillet set over medium-high heat. When it's hot, add the shrimp and tomato, and season with salt and pepper. Cook for 2 to 3 minutes, just until the shrimp are barely pink and opaque—just done (they'll continue to cook a bit, and then even more when they hit the hot pasta). Transfer the shrimp and tomatoes to a plate or tray, and don't wipe out the pan.

Add another drizzle of olive oil to the pan, and reduce the heat to medium. Add the onion, celery, and thyme and sauté for 4 to 5 minutes. Season lightly with salt and pepper and add the garlic. Cook for 30 seconds more. Add the chowder and ¼ cup Parmesan and stir to combine.

Using a handheld blender or an upright blender, blend the sauce until it's mostly smooth (I like a little texture, but you do you). Transfer the sauce back to the pan, if needed. Reduce the heat to medium-low and bring the mixture to a gentle simmer while you make the pasta.

Prepare the linguine in salted water to al dente according to package directions. Reserve ¾ cup of the starchy water after cooking.

Transfer the cooked pasta directly into the clam sauce (tongs work great here) along with about ½ cup of that starchy liquid. Toss to coat the pasta. Add the shrimp and tomatoes and season with additional salt and lots of pepper. Serve topped with extra Parmesan, some chopped basil or parsley, and a drizzle of olive oil.

Note: Clam chowder also makes a great topping for baked potatoes, or as the base for a seafood pie filling.

Fried-Rice Paella

SERVES 4 TO 6

APPROXIMATE TIME: 45 MINUTES

2 tablespoons olive oil, plus more as needed

8 ounces Spanish style chorizo, thinly sliced (salami can be subbed, not Mexican chorizo—see Note)

1 small yellow onion, diced

1 pint cherry tomatoes

2 tablespoons paprika

1 teaspoon smoked paprika (optional)

2 teaspoons dried oregano

Salt

Freshly ground black pepper

3 garlic cloves, minced

¼ cup sherry (or more, if you like it a bit stronger)

20 ounces frozen chicken fried rice

1 pound medium to large uncooked shrimp, peeled and deveined, tails on or off

Serving suggestions: fresh parsley, a drizzle of good olive oil, and spicy, store-bought chipotle mayo with a little garlic powder added. You can also make a quick-fix "aioli" by stirring together ¾ cup mayonnaise, 1 teaspoon garlic powder, and tomato paste to taste. Thin with olive oil, if you like.

Using a bag of frozen chicken fried rice to springboard your way into paella territory is one of my favorite time-saving tricks in this book. Sure, you're not going to end up with some perfectly authentic Spanish paella, but the results do bear a deliciously tasty resemblance. This recipe contains multitudes, as it not only grants permission to skip several steps via the help of a frozen product, but it also says, "it's fine, go ahead and use the bottle of 'cooking' sherry." If you want to purchase a fancy bottle of drinking sherry, by all means go for it. But the notion that you should only cook with wines that you would drink isn't necessarily something we have to cling to so tightly, all of the time. I tested both an inexpensive bottle of cooking sherry in this recipe, as well as a pricier bottle of sipping sherry, and the difference was negligible. While not traditional, I love the latent sweetness it lends—it totally makes the dish. But please use what you feel like paying for and do it without guilt or shame.

Adjust the oven rack to the middle position, and preheat to 400 degrees F.

Heat the olive oil in a large, deep oven-safe skillet or paella pan (if you have one) set over medium heat. Add the chorizo, onion, tomatoes, paprika, smoked paprika (if using) and oregano. Cook, stirring occasionally, for 6 to 7 minutes, until the sausage is crispy and the tomatoes have burst. Season with salt and pepper. Add the garlic and cook, stirring, for 30 seconds more.

Add the sherry and let it simmer, stirring frequently, for 5 to 7 minutes, cooking it down until it's almost totally evaporated. Add the fried rice and cook, stirring, until it's well mixed and totally thawed.

Toss the shrimp with a couple teaspoons of olive oil and season with salt and pepper. Arrange them over the top of the rice as evenly as possible, and bake for 7 to 10 minutes, just until the shrimp is cooked through, depending on how large your shrimp is.

Serve with freshly chopped parsley, a drizzle of extra olive oil, and/or some chipotle mayo or tomato aioli, if you like (see serving suggestions).

Notes: Many bags of frozen fried rice come with packets of sauce or flavoring. We don't need it for this recipe, but you can save it in the freezer to use in so many different things, like in the Cold Soba Noodles with

Sprouts and Edamame (page 119). Or use it as a marinade for almost any protein you see fit.

Spanish chorizo is quite different from Mexican chorizo, as it is dried and cured, whereas Mexican chorizo is sold raw and features a different blend of spices and flavorings. Spanish chorizo is often available near the cured meats in the deli section/ case, typically near things you'd use on a charcuterie board. Raw or "bulk" Mexican-style chorizo won't work as well in this application, so if you are unable to find the Spanish variety, I'd recommend substituting a nice salami or even a summer sausage, as they will best replicate the texture here.

Baja Fish Tacos

I've mentioned a few times throughout this book how these recipes are intended to stand as permission slips of sorts. Acting as supportive pages of approval—from me in my kitchen to you in yours—I'm essentially urging you to go right ahead and abandon any and all feelings of pressure to "be the best." No, we're all just out here doing our best, aren't we? Recipes that lead with intimidation and pretentiousness, with hard-to-find or pricey ingredients, need not apply here. Recipes whose directions come with so many steps that they feel like more of a climb are not at all the point. We're aiming for joy in these pages, the kind that meets you where you are, no climbing steps required. These tacos? They use frozen crispy battered fish fillets and a doctored bagged coleslaw. They are easy. They are incredibly fast to prepare. They are delicious and incidentally, one of my very favorite, joy-filled things.

SERVES 4 (2 TACOS PER PERSON, WITH
   A COUPLE OF EXTRAS)
APPROXIMATE TIME: 15 TO 20 MINUTES

1 (16-ounce) bag coleslaw

**3 scallions, white and green
   parts, chopped**

1 teaspoon garlic powder

**1 cup chopped fresh cilantro,
   plus more for topping**

Juice of 1 lime

**1 cup mayonnaise, divided, plus
   more as needed**

Salt

Freshly ground black pepper

**1 tablespoon hot sauce, plus
   more to taste**

8 to 12 corn tortillas, warmed

**10 frozen crispy beer-battered
   fish fillets, heated per
   package directions (see Note)**

**Serving suggestions: sliced
   avocado, cut limes for
   squeezing over**

In a large bowl, combine the coleslaw, chopped scallions, garlic powder, cilantro, lime juice, and about ½ cup of mayo. Season with salt and pepper and toss thoroughly until well combined. Taste and adjust any ingredients as you like (ex: add more mayo if you like a creamier slaw, etc.)

Combine the remaining ½ cup of mayo and the hot sauce (use as much as you like) and stir until blended.

To build the tacos, spread some of the creamy hot sauce onto each tortilla and top with a hot piece of crispy fish. Pile some slaw on top and nestle in a couple of slices of avocado, if desired. Serve with extra cilantro and fresh limes, if desired.

Note: The frozen fish industry has really come a long way since the early 1990s, when I ate my weight in fish sticks. Now, high-quality, sustainable choices are available at every major supermarket, and they usually come with a few options. I like the beer-battered variety for this, as they're perfect for a classic Baja-style taco. But feel free to select what sounds good to you. You should also know that premade coconut shrimp work really well here, too.

Creamy Garlic Butter Corn and Salmon Bite Bowls

If you aren't so much into corn, I'd probably suggest skipping this one. But if you're anything like me and adore the stuff, then go ahead and zoom in, because we're not messing around. A bed of creamy quick-cooking polenta is topped with a simple yet highly flavorful corn sauce (yes, a corn sauce) and then finished with my favorite way to wield some simple salmon fillets. These salmon "bites" cook quickly, and thanks to their more diminutive stature, they are better primed to char and crisp up under the broiler. Transforming a simple can of cream-style corn into a truly drool-worthy sauce is an easy trick, and makes for a perfectly luscious topping. Doubling down on the corn here just makes sense, and it also makes for a delicious, flavor-packed bowl of pure sunshine.

SERVES 4

APPROXIMATE TIME: 30 MINUTES

2 tablespoons olive oil, plus more for drizzling and as needed

4 tablespoons butter, divided

1 shallot, minced

3 garlic cloves, minced

1 to 2 red chiles, sliced (optional)

1 cup frozen, canned, or fresh corn kernels

Salt

Freshly ground black pepper

1 (15-ounce) can cream-style corn

1 to 1½ cups milk, half-and-half, or coconut milk, divided

1 cup instant polenta or grits

4 cups vegetable or chicken stock

4 skinless salmon fillets

Serving suggestions: Simple Arugula Salad (page 86) or fresh green herbs and/or arugula

Adjust the oven rack to the top position, and preheat the broiler to high.

Heat 2 tablespoons of olive oil and 2 tablespoons of butter in a large skillet set over medium heat. When the butter has melted, add the shallot, garlic, chiles, and corn and cook for 1 to 2 minutes. Season with salt and pepper.

Add the cream-style corn to the pan and stir. Reduce the heat to low, add ½ to ⅔ cup of milk and let the sauce simmer lightly, stirring occasionally, while you prepare the polenta and salmon.

For the polenta, cook it according to the package directions, using the stock instead of water. When it's cooked (usually takes about 5 minutes), add the remaining ½ to 1 cup (depending on how creamy you want it) of milk. Add the remaining 2 tablespoons of butter and allow it to melt into the mixture.

Cut the salmon fillets into bite-size pieces (you should get about 8 bites per fillet, depending on the exact size you purchase). Spray a baking sheet with nonstick spray or lightly brush with oil. Transfer the salmon bites to the baking sheet, drizzle with olive oil to coat, and season with salt and pepper. Broil for 7 to 8 minutes, or until just done.

To serve, spoon some polenta into each of 4 individual bowls and top with some of the creamy corn sauce. Finish with the salmon bites and the Simple Arugula Salad or just plain chopped herbs and/or arugula.

Honey-Miso Swordfish Skewers

Three powerhouse ingredients—miso, honey, and lime—come together in what I think is about the tastiest combination to ever grace a piece of swordfish. The point of this recipe is to highlight the meaty, flavorful fish with just a few simple things (pantry things, really, as I think everyone should have miso around) and then serve it up in a fun, less-expected way. Or, maybe you do expect food on a stick at your dinner table, but I can tell you that my own family tends to light up when I set things like this down. You can do this with just about any fish you like (tuna also works well), but I like the meaty, heartiness of swordfish, a fish that just so happens to sport a built-in skewer, so it's really just fitting all around. My mind doesn't always drift to skewers on a weeknight at dinnertime, but every time I do happen to remember how delicious these are, and how they actually manage to get my picky-eater-child-who-shall-not-be-named to inhale an entire piece of fish, I'm always glad to have had such a happy eureka moment.

SERVES 4

APPROXIMATE TIME: 1 HOUR

8 wooden skewers

2 tablespoons white miso

1 tablespoon honey

Juice of 1 lime, plus more for drizzling

1 tablespoon olive oil

4 (6-ounce) swordfish fillets, cut into bite-size pieces (thawed if frozen)

Freshly chopped cilantro and scallion greens, or A Friendly Herb Salad, Southeast Asian version (page 86)

Serving suggestions: serve over rice or in tortillas or pita bread; wrap in lettuce leaves.

Soak the skewers in water (they'll still blacken under the broiler, but this will keep them from burning up). Alternatively, you can skip the skewers and serve swordfish bites, which works just as well.

Combine the miso, honey, lime juice, and olive oil in a large dish. Put the swordfish pieces in the marinade and toss them around, evenly coating each piece. Marinate in the fridge for at least 30 minutes. (The small amount of lime juice won't "cook" the fish, creating a ceviche situation, if you were wondering.)

Preheat the broiler to high, and adjust the rack to the top position. Grease a baking sheet with a little oil or nonstick spray (parchment paper tends to scorch).

Thread 4 or 5 pieces of fish on each skewer and place them on the prepared baking sheet. Broil the skewers for 8 to 10 minutes, until charred on top and just cooked through, no need to flip.

Enjoy these in tacos, in a rice bowl, or as a lovely little lettuce wrap moment. Tuck them inside some pita bread or, as I tend to do, squeeze a little more lime on them, shower them with fresh herbs (cilantro and scallions, usually) and serve them right on their skewers.

Tiny Tuna and Tomato Melts

I love a good tuna melt almost any way I can get it. Served open-faced, all toasty with melted cheese, piled between two slices of crusty, seedy bread, or—in this case—as small handheld tartlets. During a recent social media scrolling, I happened to catch a glimpse of someone making small tomato pies and my Southern heart skipped a beat at the notion of the beloved summertime treat being reimagined in miniature. I've taken the same idea down that road just a little further, pulling tuna, capers, and spicy pickled jalapeños along for the ride. All told, these things are little flavor bombs—they're quite hearty and they pack a serious punch. I like to enjoy two or three with a simple salad on the side as a unique warm-weather meal that crams a lot of flavor into a relatively small package. The crusts are made from crushed chive and onion sandwich crackers, but you could absolutely skip that and just pile the creamy tuna mixture onto a thick slice of bread or split English muffins, top with tomatoes and cheese and then broil until you can't stand waiting one more minute.

MAKES 12 TARTS

APPROXIMATE TIME: 35 MINUTES

24 chive-and-onion sandwich crackers

4 tablespoons olive oil or melted butter

20 ounces canned tuna, of choice, drained

¼ cup mayonnaise

1 tablespoon spicy brown mustard

¼ cup capers, drained

¼ cup chopped pickled jalapeños or dill pickles

¼ teaspoon garlic powder

2 cups shredded cheddar cheese, divided

Freshly ground black pepper

Salt

2 Roma tomatoes, thinly sliced

Preheat the oven to 350 degrees F. Spray 12 muffin cups with nonstick spray.

Combine the sandwich crackers and olive oil in a food processor and pulse until the mixture resembles wet sand. You can add a little extra oil or butter if it seems dry. Evenly divide the mixture between the 12 muffin cups and lightly press it down, flattening the bottoms and then working it up the sides a bit, creating shallow cups.

Bake the cups for 10 minutes while you prepare the filling.

In a bowl, combine the tuna, mayo, mustard, capers, jalapeños, garlic powder, and about 1 cup of shredded cheddar. Stir to combine. Taste and adjust as needed, seasoning with pepper and a little salt (though it probably won't need it).

Divide the mixture between the cups, gently pressing it down to create even tops. Top each cup with a tomato slice and about 1 tablespoon or so of cheese. Bake for about 15 minutes, until the cheese is melted and bubbly. Allow the tartlets to cool for at least 10 to 15 minutes before removing them (they will firm up and become easier to handle).

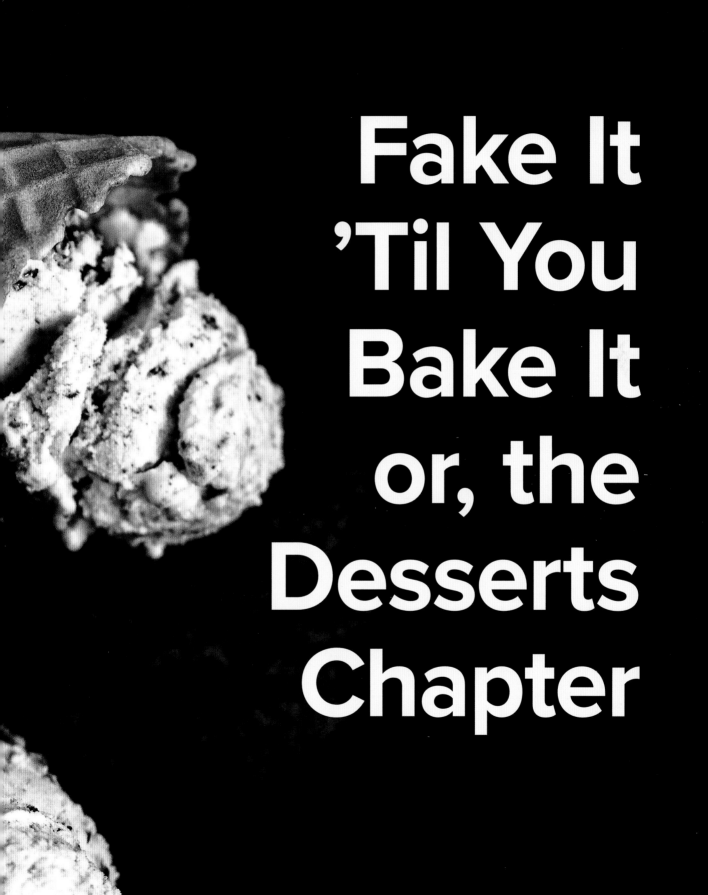

Fake It 'Til You Bake It

or, the Desserts Chapter

Blueberry-Lemon Cornbread Cookies

This is a real sleeper recipe, let me tell you. In my chocolate-loving household, these unassuming cookies sneakily swept in and stole everyone's hearts. A simple box of corn muffin mix changes direction, mid-preparation, taking a sharp turn toward the dessert table, thanks to the addition of tangy lemon curd and luscious brown butter. I set a plate of them on the counter one afternoon, curious to see how they'd fare. Not only were they devoured within 10 minutes of landing there, but they were met with total and utter joy. That's the best thing, right? For home cooks and bakers anyway. When people genuinely love what you've made, when it makes them happy . . . even if it's from a mix. Most love of good food isn't conditional; it doesn't hinge on everything being prepared a certain way or with specific ingredients. Delicious is as delicious does. It's really as simple as that.

MAKES ABOUT 9 COOKIES
APPROXIMATE TIME: 35 MINUTES

1 (8.5-ounce) box corn muffin mix

2 tablespoons flour

¼ cup butter

¼ cup granulated sugar

1 tablespoon lemon curd

⅓ cup frozen wild blueberries, no need to thaw

Adjust the oven rack to the middle position, and preheat to 325 degrees F.

Whisk the corn muffin mix and flour together in a large bowl.

Melt the butter in a saucepan over medium heat. Continue cooking the butter for about 2 minutes more, until it appears golden and smells nutty. Remove the pan from the heat and stir in the sugar and lemon curd.

Pour the butter mixture into the bowl with the flour mixture, add 1 tablespoon of water, and stir gently until just combined and no dry bits remain. Add the blueberries and stir gently to mix them evenly throughout the dough (some will probably break, smash, or burst on you, which is totally fine).

Form the mixture into 1½-inch (give or take) balls and space them evenly on a baking sheet. Bake for 20 to 25 minutes, until golden brown and crisped around the edges. Allow the cookies to cool for at least 5 minutes before transferring them to a cooling rack. When stored in a covered container, these will keep at room temperature for up to 4 days.

Note: Frozen wild blueberries tend to be smaller, which makes them perfect for cookies. You'll have a lot left over, but they're incredibly useful in so many things. They're especially great in muffins, pancakes, waffles, and smoothies.

Salted Apple Butter–Apple Pandowdy with Crème Fraîche

I'm on this not-so-secret mission to get people to use more sour cream in and on their desserts. It's fantastic as a cool and creamy topping on so many sweet things, from chocolate cake and towering trifles to this apple pandowdy. My husband thought it sounded awful and advised that I tell people to use crème fraîche, so that's what I'm doing—that's how we're labeling things here. But just know that even though I'm listing crème fraîche as the topper for this apple dessert, I'm actually hoping you try sour cream. They're both perfect with this, as the inherent sweetness of the sugar cookie crust begs for the balance offered by the sour cream. It's a total match made in heaven, and one of the easiest baked apple desserts you will ever make. Oh, and Lucas did end up trying it with sour cream and said it was "actually really great." So, there's that.

SERVES 6 TO 8
APPROXIMATE TIME: 1 HOUR

5 Granny Smith apples sliced paper-thin (no need to peel; see Note)

¾ cup apple butter

½ teaspoon salt

1 (16-ounce) package prepared sugar cookie dough

Turbinado sugar (optional), for sprinkling

8 ounces crème fraîche (ahem, or sour cream!)

Adjust an oven rack to the bottom position, and preheat to 400 degrees F.

Combine the apples, apple butter, and salt in a 9 x 13-inch baking dish and toss to thoroughly mix. You're looking for a salted, not salty, flavor—like salted caramel. So, add a little more salt until you get there.

Create a crust by flattening and pressing the cookie dough all over the top of the apples, making a smooth layer. It's okay if it doesn't reach to the edges of the dish, it will expand a bit and you're going to slice it all up anyway. Just get it as flat and evenly spread as you can. Sprinkle with a few teaspoons of turbinado sugar for a sparkly crust, if you like.

Bake for 30 to 35 minutes, or until the crust is a beautiful golden brown.

Remove from the oven and cut long slashes down through the crust every couple of inches or so. Dollop some of the crème fraîche (or sour cream!) all over, using as much as you like, so it can sink and melt down into those crevices you just created via your knife-imposed natural disaster. Enjoy warm.

Notes: The "paper-thin" apples directive here is best achieved via the use of a mandoline, which may go against my no single-use kitchen items rule, but it's worth having one. They are quite inexpensive and easy to find, and they save so much prep time that they're worth the exception.

Need a use for any extra apple butter? Try shaking up a tablespoon or so with a classic Old Fashioned cocktail recipe for a sweetly spiced twist.

Oatmeal Crumble Peach Cobbler with Cinnamon-Sugar Biscuits

We've unofficially settled on the unofficial name "crumbler" for this indecisive entry in this chapter o' desserts. I'm not totally sure which confectionary camp it wants to claim—crisp? or cobbler? This recipe hovers somewhere right in the middle, walking the line between both. For this reason, I think it's my favorite sweet recipe in this book, because it's a little bit of an oddball. But why just crumble when you can also cobbler? Inspired by both the crispy peach cobbler in Renee Erickson's *A Boat, a Whale, and a Walrus* as well as a peach crisp-cobbler recipe by the amazing nineteenth-century Southern cookbook author Abby Fisher, this hybrid recipe is so simple it's silly. We're going to take a shortcut via some oatmeal cookie mix, turning it into the perfect crumbly topping. We'll also roll some flaky biscuits in a little cinnamon sugar, giving this dish a topographically intriguing surface that is the perfect landing place for some cold, creamy vanilla ice cream. That said, if you prefer you can absolutely go with one or the other here—either the cookie crisp topping or the spiced, sweet biscuits.

SERVES 6 TO 8
APPROXIMATE TIME: < 1 HOUR

4 (15-ounce) cans peach slices, not drained (in fruit juice, not syrup)

8 tablespoons butter, at room temperature

1 (17- to 18-ounce) package oatmeal cookie mix

¼ to ½ teaspoon salt

1 (16.3-ounce) can flaky biscuits

2 tablespoons granulated sugar

½ teaspoon ground cinnamon

Serving suggestion: vanilla ice cream or frozen yogurt

Adjust the oven rack to the middle position, and preheat to 375 degrees F.

Pour the peaches and their juices in a 9 x 13-inch baking dish.

In a large bowl, combine the butter with the oatmeal cookie mix and a pinch of salt, and mix with your hands, creating a crumbly topping. Work the mixture until the butter is fully incorporated. Scatter this all over the peaches.

Cut the biscuits in half (or quarters or leave them whole!) and roll them into balls. Transfer them to a large bowl, add the cinnamon and sugar, and toss them until they are coated evenly. Arrange them on top of the oatmeal crumble.

Bake for about 45 minutes, or until bubbly and the biscuits are deeply golden brown. If the biscuits brown too much before the insides are cooked, lay a large piece of aluminum foil over the top to slow that down. Serve with vanilla ice cream or frozen yogurt.

Ritzies

This recipe is what one might call "a hack." It tastes a whole lot like my very favorite Girl Scout cookie, a fact that I gleefully discovered when I first made them for my kids. Upon learning that, I now make them mostly to calm my own cravings, though I do share with the other members of my household. This is the sort of recipe that needs no strict measurements or amounts—it's so straightforward, so very casual by design that I almost feel silly telling you how many sandwich crackers to use. So, I'm calling it an un-recipe. Really, you should make as few or as many as you like. You could select a single sandwich cracker, coat it in a tablespoon of melted chocolate, shower it with sprinkles if you want, and call it good. The point is that I make the introduction. The point is that you know this is a thing. Now that you do, whether or not to share is totally up to you . . . .

MAKE(S) AS MANY AS YOU WANT AND/
    OR NEED
APPROXIMATE TIME: < 5 MINUTES

**Peanut butter sandwich
    crackers**

**Chocolate chips, melted per
    package instructions**

**Rainbow sprinkles (totally
    optional, but highly
    recommended)**

Coat the sandwich crackers in melted chocolate, allowing any excess to drip off. Place them on a flat surface and sprinkle generously with sprinkles (ha!). Allow them to set completely before enjoying or storing.

They will keep in a covered airtight container at room temperature for up to a week.

Crushed Mandarin Sundaes with Sesame Caramel and Pistachios

Like a remixed, grownup take on a Dreamsicle, these sundaes are a testament to the fact that sometimes—nay, most of the time—it's the thought that counts. We're not making a single thing from scratch here folks. It's store-bought caramel that we're going to bippity-boppity-boo into a more magical, delicious version of itself. Sesame oil, a true pantry staple ingredient, and a little more salt do the trick. The nutty, come-hither aroma of sesame oil is absolutely perfect with the sweet caramel and the juicy citrus. Of course you can use fresh mandarins, but the juiciness of the canned or jarred variety is nice here. Salty pistachios give these unique sundaes just the right amount of crunch and color. Sometimes great home cooking is more about selecting interesting ingredients and combining them in fresh, new ways. These sundaes fit the bill, and then some.

SERVES 4

APPROXIMATE TIME: 10 MINUTES

1 cup store-bought salted caramel

½ teaspoon sesame oil, or as needed

Salt

Vanilla ice cream

16 ounces canned mandarin orange segments, drained and lightly crushed

½ cup salted shelled pistachios, coarsely chopped

Combine the caramel and sesame oil in a small saucepan over medium-low heat. Simmer gently for about 5 minutes. Remove the pan from the heat and pop it in the fridge until it's cool enough to taste. Add a little more salt, if needed (most store-bought salted caramels aren't salty enough).

Create your sundaes by scooping some vanilla ice cream into serving bowls and topping with the juicy crushed mandarin segments, a sprinkling of chopped pistachios, and a generous drizzle of the warm sesame caramel.

Olive Oil–Crisped Pound Cake with Vanilla-Basil Sugar

Like a trick of the light or a really flattering mirror, a recipe's delicious beginnings can grow right out of the name we assign it. I know, how shallow of me, right? But, it's still true. They say we eat with our eyes first, but that's not quite right, I don't think. No, it's our ears that get to the food first, parsing and sorting the recipe's name, evaluating and analyzing whether or not it's going to be a flop or a win. Before we ever smell, taste, touch, or gaze upon a dish, be it at a restaurant or in our own kitchen, chances are we're going to encounter the name first. So, words matter. Names make a difference. They have the power to excite and entice, to intrigue or even repel. Don't believe me? Just ask meatloaf. This recipe could technically be, "Pound Cake with Basil Sugar," but it just sounds so much more alluring when you add a little more oomph to it. *Olive oil-crisped . . . vanilla-basil sugar . . .* yes, that's more like it.

SERVES 4

APPROXIMATE TIME: 5 MINUTES

4 tablespoons olive oil, plus more as needed

1 (12-ounce) regular (vanilla) pound cake from your grocer's bakery, cut into ½-inch-thick slices

½ cup granulated sugar

1 heaping teaspoon basil paste or ¼ cup fresh basil leaves (see Note)

½ to ¾ teaspoon vanilla bean paste (or the seeds from 1 vanilla bean)

Heat the olive oil in a skillet set over medium heat. When it's hot, toast the pound cake slices for 1½ to 2 minutes per side, until golden brown and lightly crisped. Transfer the slices to a platter or individual serving plates.

Combine the sugar, basil paste, and the vanilla bean paste in a food processor and pulse until well mixed (it will somewhat resemble wet sand). Pile this on top of each toasted cake slice upon serving, using as much as you like.

Note: Quality fresh basil isn't available everywhere all of the time, and this recipe acknowledges that. The paste works beautifully, though you may remain unconvinced at first. But just trust it. The final flavor, combined with the sweet sugar and vanilla, is just as it should be. If you prefer to use fresh, combine the sugar, ¼ cup fresh basil leaves, and the vanilla bean paste in a food processor, and process until well combined.

Cinnamon-Oatmeal Cookie Ice Cream

This flavor combo remains my very favorite ice cream of all time (no big deal). It's a total dupe for a Ben and Jerry's flavor that, I believe, was discontinued and then recontinued but in this very elusive, hard-to-find way. I used to go to the store, mosey into the "ice cream and novelties" aisle with this pitiful sense of desperation, hoping that they'd finally have it in stock, this amazing flavor I loved so much. But honestly? That was for the birds. So, I began a very "homemade-ish" approach to my ice creaming after that, as I also didn't have nor did I care to procure an ice cream maker (storage issues). I took matters into my own kitchen and just started making this version, and my cones and sundaes have been all the better for it, ever since.

MAKES 48 OUNCES, BUT IS EASILY
   DIVIDED OR MULTIPLIED AS NEEDED
APPROXIMATE TIME: 10 MINUTES PLUS
   FREEZING TIME

48 ounces vanilla bean ice cream, slightly softened (see Note)

1½ teaspoons ground cinnamon

¾ to 1 cup chopped semisweet chocolate (either chips or a bar work)

3 to 4 store-bought oatmeal cookies, finely chopped

In a large bowl, stir together the softened ice cream, cinnamon, chopped chocolate, and chopped cookie bits. When it's all evenly blended, transfer the mixture into a covered freezer-safe container and freeze until firm.

Note: By no means do you have to stick to the amounts that I've listed here. You can whip up a single serving of this if you like, or transform a whole container of vanilla ice cream into something new and exciting. Also? You don't really need to measure these things. Just add a little of each thing until the ice cream tastes amazing **to you**.

Double Smashed Raspberry Fools

Quite possibly the easiest dessert ever, a fool is little more than fruit that is swirled into or piled atop some freshly whipped custard or cream. There's freedom in this dessert, I think. It's demonstrating the happy fact that you really don't have to overthink or overcomplicate things, especially where sweets are concerned. It's almost like someone was going to make ice cream sundaes for a party but totally forgot the ice cream, leaving nothing but saucy sweet fruit and cream to enjoy. A happy accident by all accounts (this totally fake scenario I've just described), because it turns out that the utterly simple combination of fruit and cream is delicious, its plain-Jane appearance fooling us into thinking that it's not going to be much of anything. But one jammy, cloudlike spoonful of this stuff, and you'll see that these little fools are in fact, exactly everything.

SERVES 4 TO 6

APPROXIMATE TIME: < 10 MINUTES

1 pint fresh raspberries

3 tablespoons framboise, optional (raspberry liqueur, this accounts for the first "smashing")

2 teaspoons granulated sugar

2 teaspoons vanilla bean paste or vanilla extract, divided

Pinch of salt

1 pint heavy whipping cream

¼ cup powdered sugar

Combine the berries, framboise (as much of this as you like), sugar, 1 teaspoon of vanilla, and a pinch of salt in a bowl and mash them up a bit with a fork (the second smashing). Let this sit while you make the whipped cream.

Combine the cream, powdered sugar, and the remaining 1 teaspoon of vanilla to the bowl of a stand mixer or mixing bowl (using a handheld mixer) and whip on high speed for 3 or 4 minutes, until stiff peaks form.

Serve the fools by dolloping big piles of whipped cream into serving bowls or plates and spooning some of the sweetened vanilla berries all over top. Alternatively, you can layer this in glasses.

Honey-Roasted Pears with Rosemary-Pecan Crumble

If you were to close your eyes while enjoying this little pear number, you might just mistake it for a pie. But it couldn't be simpler to make and the "wow" factor is off the charts—a true high-impact, low-effort situation (the very best kind). The buttery, honey roasted pears do their slow collapsing in the oven, getting all soft and even sweeter than they began. This alone makes for a pretty nice treat, to be honest. But I've found that by simply whirling up a package of store-bought glazed pecans with some fresh rosemary, you get this incredibly delicious crumbly, crunchy topping that is great on so many things. But nothing more so than these pears. Because let's be honest—pears and rosemary and pecans are a wintry trio that are just meant to be together. Vanilla ice cream is optional but completes the scene beautifully.

SERVES 4

APPROXIMATE TIME: <30 MINUTES

4 ripe pears, any kind, cored and halved (no need to peel)

2 tablespoons butter, melted

2 tablespoons honey

1 tablespoon balsamic vinegar

¼ teaspoon freshly ground black pepper

¼ cup fresh rosemary leaves

1 cup store-bought glazed pecans

Serving suggestions: vanilla ice cream or crème fraîche

Adjust the oven rack to the middle position, and preheat to 375 degrees F.

Transfer the pear halves skin-side down to an 8 x 10-inch baking dish. In a bowl, combine the melted butter, honey, vinegar, and black pepper and mix well. Pour the mixture all over the pears and roast for 15 minutes.

Meanwhile, combine the rosemary and glazed pecans in a food processor. Process just until the mixture almost resembles wet sand—it should be pretty finely ground. Just don't overmix or you'll end up with pecan butter (delicious, but not the texture we're going for).

Serve the warm, honey-roasted pears with this rosemary-pecan crumble on top, just piled as high as you like. Vanilla ice cream or crème fraîche are also really great with this.

Pineapple–Poppy Seed Tart

While this recipe resembles a classic French *tarte tatin*, I'm not going to call it that for two reasons. Firstly, that fancy-leaning moniker carries a bit of an intimidation factor—I don't want to deter you right out of the gate. Tartes are the leading experts in their field, the field of "foods that seem very difficult to make but are actually very easy." There may be no more satisfying type of cooking, honestly, than recipes that trick your guests (or even, somehow, yourself) into thinking that you invested far more into their preparation than you actually did. You can't beat that. Secondly? This is a very saucy thing, this tart, a bit more so than your average tatin. So, I'm going with just "tart." A bright and cheery shingling of juicy pineapples gives a definite nod to the classic upside-down cake as well. The delightful micro-crunch from the poppy seeds makes the finished confection look like the prettiest night sky, only with its colors in reverse.

MAKES ONE 10-INCH TART
APPROXIMATE TIME: 50 MINUTES

5 tablespoons butter

¾ cup loosely packed brown sugar

Pinch of salt

2 tablespoons poppy seeds

1 fresh pineapple, cored or 1 (15-ounce) can pineapple rings, drained

1 sheet frozen puff pastry, thawed

Serving suggestion: lightly sweetened sour cream or crème fraîche

Adjust the oven rack to the middle position, and preheat to 350 degrees F. Spray a 9-inch nonstick cake pan with nonstick cooking spray.

Combine the butter, brown sugar, salt, and poppy seeds in a large skillet over medium heat. Allow the butter to completely melt and the sugar to dissolve. Pour this mixture into the 9-inch cake pan.

If using a fresh pineapple, cut it into ½-inch-thick rings. Shingle the slices in the pan, nestling them into the brown sugar mixture.

Cut the pastry to fit in the pan (doesn't need to be or look perfect) and place it on top of the pineapple, tucking and sealing the sides to fit as best you can. Bake for about 30 minutes, until very golden brown. Let it rest for 10 minutes before trying to invert.

To invert the tart, run a sharp knife around the edges to loosen, place a large plate or dish over the pan and holding the plate and pan together, flip it over, allowing the whole tart and all of that sauce to slip and slide onto the plate. If this doesn't happen for you, no worries! Just keep it in the pan and slice it there, flipping each slice over as you place it on the plate. No harm, no foul.

Serve with lightly sweetened sour cream or crème fraîche, if you like.

Note: This is optional, but I love the balancing act of barely sweetened sour cream with any supersweet dessert (like this one). I just sweeten some sour cream to taste with either honey, maple syrup, or even some of the brown sugar from the dish and dollop a bit on the slices of warm tart.

Cookies and Cream

This recipe reads a little funny, I'll admit it. We're just dipping store-bought crispy chocolate chip cookies into milk and then layering them with some freshly whipped cream and whatever crunchy thing strikes your fancy. Simple as it is, what you'll end up with is absolutely greater than the sum of its parts. You get this trifle of sorts, a word that literally means "unimportant thing." In this case, the name definitely does not fit the recipe, at least not in the literal sense. I can attest to the fact that, though this particular cohort of ingredients is small and somewhat unassuming, when you combine them in this way they really do put on a show. The cookies get soft and airy, convening with the vanilla-scented freshly whipped cream in a way that, if you're at all like the people in my household, will elicit actual, real-deal wonder. No kidding.

MAKES 4 INDIVIDUAL SERVINGS
APPROXIMATE TIME: 30 MINUTES

1 pint heavy whipping cream

2 heaping tablespoons powdered sugar

1 teaspoon vanilla extract

1 cup milk

12 crispy chocolate chip cookies

¼ to ½ cup crunchy bits such as chopped chocolate chips, chopped toffee bars, chopped salty peanuts, whatever you like

Using either a handheld mixer or a stand mixer, whip the cream in a large bowl on high speed until soft peaks form. Add the powdered sugar and vanilla, and whip until stiff peaks form.

Spoon a small bit of whipped cream to each of 4 serving glasses (I use clear rocks glasses for this). Pour the milk into a bowl and dip a cookie in it, fully submerging it and getting it nice and soaked. Put the cookie on top of the whipped cream and then put more whipped cream on top of that cookie. Repeat until each glass has 3 cookies, ending with a big dollop of whipped cream. Top each glass with some of the crunchy bits you've chosen and enjoy.

These can be made in advance (the cookies are meant to soften) and will last for 2 to 3 days in the refrigerator, lightly covered if possible.

Chocolate-Hazelnut Creme with Speculoos Dust

Chocolate-hazelnut spread is just such a wonderful thing and from what I can tell, it tends to conjure nothing but glee from those who taste it. So we're going to swoosh and swirl it into a heap of cloudlike cream—technically this is called a "creme" and it is a close relative to a "fool" (see page 209). We'll then shower the fluffy peaks with what I'm calling a "dust." This is another example of how the naming of a recipe is half the fun sometimes, as we discussed on page 207. This is almost an un-recipe, and it's a solid way to satisfy a craving for pie without having to actually make a pie. No baking, no excessive equipment, just a pan and a mixer and a hungry heart is all you need to make the greatest wanna-be pie there ever was.

MAKES 4 (1-CUP) SERVINGS
APPROXIMATE TIME: < 15 MINUTES

1 pint cold heavy whipping cream

¾ cup chocolate-hazelnut spread (such as Nutella)

10 to 12 speculoos cookies, crushed into a dust (such as Biscoff)

Pour the cream into the bowl of a stand mixer fitted with the whisk attachment (or use a mixing bowl and a hand mixer). Whip on medium speed for 60 seconds, until soft peaks form.

Add the chocolate-hazelnut spread and whisk on high for about 1 minute, until stiff peaks form (be careful not to over-whip it, as then you will have made butter which isn't really the goal).

Serve the creme with the cookie dust sprinkled on top. The creme can be stored for up to 3 days, covered, in the refrigerator.

Flavor spin-offs: Swap lemon or orange curd in for the chocolate-hazelnut spread and use Nilla wafers or graham crackers for the "dust." Or, try peanut butter mousse and use crushed chocolate wafers or even crispy chocolate chip cookies as the topping. There is such a thing as speculoos butter which, of course, is perfect here.

Peanut Butter Burnt Basque Cheesecake

Hailing from Spain's beautiful Basque country, there's nothing homemade-ish about this recipe. It's fully homemade, through and through. But I'm sharing it here because it's the easiest cheesecake recipe you'll ever make, and also the fastest—both qualities that fit so nicely with our goals for this recipe book. Sporting a menacing, almost grumpy-seeming face that only a mother could love, this dessert seems to occupy a confectionery space all its own. The fact that it is supposed to be very dark—near burnt, actually—ushers this fresh breeze of ease and comfort into the baking process that makes it much more fun. Furthermore, it creates its own crust, preventing us from having to fuss with that. The peanut butter element here makes that crust taste almost like peanut butter cookies (a lovely bonus). And I'd be lying if I said that pouring warm berry jam all over the top of this cake didn't completely fill my heart, satisfying my never-say-die craving for peanut butter and jelly, a universally beloved flavor pairing that never, ever grows old, no matter how much we do.

MAKES 1 (10-INCH) CHEESECAKE,
    SERVES 10 TO 12
APPROXIMATE TIME: 1 HOUR 40
    MINUTES

3½ (8-ounce) blocks cream
    cheese (28 ounces), at
    room temperature

¾ cup creamy peanut butter

2 cups granulated sugar

5 eggs, at room temperature

2 teaspoons vanilla extract

1 teaspoon salt

⅓ cup all-purpose flour

Topping suggestions: Warmed
    seedless strawberry or
    raspberry jam, honey, warm
    chocolate sauce or hot fudge

Adjust the oven rack to the middle position, and preheat to 400 degrees F. Grease a 10-inch springform pan with butter.

In the bowl of a stand mixer fitted with the whisk attachment (or in a mixing bowl using a handheld mixer), whisk the cream cheese, peanut butter, and sugar together for about 3 minutes, until smooth and creamy.

Add the eggs, one at a time, mixing in between until just combined. Add the vanilla and salt, mixing until combined. Sift the flour over the bowl and mix just until combined and no lumps remain. Pour the batter into the prepared pan and place the pan on a baking sheet (to catch any spillage, if necessary). Bake for 1 hour or until the top is deeply browned (just shy of blackened) and the center is baked but still jiggly. It will sink and firm up as it cools. If it looks too dark for your liking at 45 to 50 minutes into the bake time, lay a sheet of aluminum foil over the cake to slow that down.

Cool for at least 30 minutes before trying to remove it from the pan. Serve at room temperature with any of the suggested toppings, or just as it is.

Acknowledgments

This book was nothing but a joy to write, photograph, and cook my way through. Getting to explore the homemade-ish side of the kitchen opened up this new world of recipe development that is now firmly a part of my regularly scheduled culinary programming. The spectrum of home cooking is vast and it is as deep as the cooks who populate its kitchens. This book acknowledges the easy, laid-back side where delicious things still abound, but so does practicality, efficiency, and the full acceptance of the need to keep it real sometimes. I'm grateful to the team of supportive, creative people who completely understood what I wanted to make here, and I'm beyond thankful for having been given the chance to do it.

To Michelle Branson, my editor, for being the kindest, most lovely person to make a book with. Your positivity and guidance are everything.

To Deborah Ritchken, my wonderful agent, for your feedback, wisdom, and for helping me and my books find their wings for the past eight years.

To the team at Gibbs Smith for, yet again, being so positive and abundantly supportive of my books. It's been such a pleasure to work with you—thanks for being so great at what you do.

To Lucas, Elle, and Easton—thank you over and over again for your great patience every time I dive back into a book project. You're my heart and my reason for everything. Love you.

To all of the *My Kitchen Little* and *Talking With My Mouth Full* readers—I couldn't do this without your support as well. Thanks for welcoming me into your kitchens for the past 10 years. What an amazing, beautiful time it's been.

Index

Lauren McDuffie is a cookbook author (*Smoke, Roots, Mountain, Harvest*, and *Southern Lights*), food blogger, photographer/stylist, and creator of the cooking blog *My Kitchen Little*. She is also the creator of the critically acclaimed and award-winning food blog *Harvest and Honey*, and has articles, recipes, and photography published in various forms. Originally from Lexington, Kentucky, Lauren now lives in Portland, Oregon, with her husband and two children.

Metric Conversion Chart

Volume Measurements		Weight Measurements		Temperature	
U.S.	**Metric**	**U.S.**	**Metric**	**Fahrenheit**	**Celsius**
1 teaspoon	5 ml	½ ounce	15 g	250	120
1 tablespoon	15 ml	1 ounce	30 g	300	150
¼ cup	60 ml	3 ounces	80 g	325	160
⅓ cup	80 ml	4 ounces	115 g	350	175
½ cup	125 ml	8 ounces	225 g	375	190
⅔ cup	160 ml	12 ounces	340 g	400	200
¾ cup	180 ml	1 pound	450 g	425	220
1 cup	250 ml	2 ¼ pounds	1 kg	450	230